GRADE LEVEL

K-12

A HANDBOOK FOR TEACHERS

Effective
nstructional Strategies

VOLUME 1

Teaching

Instructional Effectiveness

Student
Achievement

Instructional Leadership

Organizational Leadership

International Center for
Leadership in Education

Rigor, Relevance, and Relationships for ALL Students

Acknowledgments

The International Center for Leadership in Education wishes to thank
the authors of this book,
Richard D. Jones, Ph.D., and Helen Branigan.

Published by International Center for
Leadership in Education, Inc.

Printed in the U.S.A.

ISBN-13: 978-1-935300-76-2

ISBN-10: 1-935300-76-8

International Center for Leadership in Education, Inc.
1587 Route 146
Rexford, New York 12148
(518) 399-2776
info@LeaderEd.com
www. LeaderEd.com

4 5 6 7 8 9 10 6710 24 23 22 21 20 19
4510006109

Contents

 # Overview

The Daggett System for Effective Instruction

The Daggett System for Effective Instruction (DSEI) provides a coherent focus across the entire education organization on the development and support of instructional effectiveness to improve student achievement. Whereas traditional teaching frameworks are teacher-focused and consider what teachers should do to deliver instruction, DSEI is student-focused and considers what the entire educational system should do to facilitate learning. It is a subtle but important difference based on current research and understanding about teaching and learning.

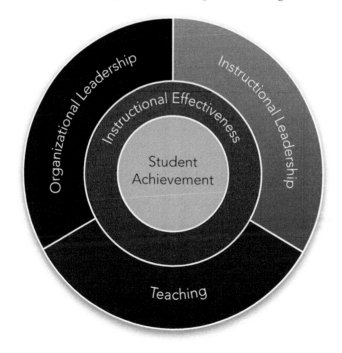

The three parts of DSEI are illustrated here. The following are the critical functions of each part of the system. Think about where you, as a professional educator, fit into this system.

Six Elements of Organizational Leadership

- Create a culture of high expectations.
- Create a shared vision.
- Build leadership capacity.
- Align organizational structures and systems to vision.
- Align teacher/administrator selection, support, and evaluation.
- Support decision making with data systems.

Five Elements of Instructional Leadership

- Use research to establish urgency for higher expectations.
- Align curriculum to standards.
- Integrate literacy and math across all content areas.
- Facilitate data-driven decision making to inform instruction.
- Provide opportunities for focused professional collaboration and growth.

Six Elements of Teaching

- Embrace rigorous and relevant expectations for all students.
- Build strong relationships with students.
- Possess depth of content knowledge and make it relevant to students.
- Facilitate rigorous and relevant instruction based on how students learn.
- Demonstrate expertise in use of instructional strategies, technology, and best practices.
- Use assessments to guide and differentiate instruction.

When all parts of the system are working together efficiently, teachers receive the support they need, and students are successfully prepared for college, careers, and citizenship.

Instructional Strategies

This handbook is a guide to help teachers expand their skill in using a variety of instructional strategies to facilitate rigorous and relevant learning. The handbook begins by explaining what the Rigor/Relevance Framework is and how it can be used to measure the rigor and relevance of curriculum, instruction, and assessment. The handbook addresses the challenges of curriculum planning and the use of various instructional strategies to enhance learning. It aligns to the DSEI through the teaching segment by including a wide variety of instructional strategies.

Finally, the teacher is provided with 17 instructional strategies, all correlated to the Rigor/Relevance Framework as well as to various types of assessment, to student learning styles, and to the use of technology.

Brainstorming

The chapter introduces this strategy by outlining helpful guidelines for implementing brainstorming in the classroom. It then presents a range of variations on brainstorming to stimulate creative thinking and problem-solving.

Cooperative Learning

This chapter explains the five basic components of cooperative learning. It then describes some effective methods of applying the strategies as well as ways in which the teacher can maximize the experience for learners.

Demonstration

This chapter defines demonstrations and explains how to prepare for and give them. Some helpful suggestions present ideas to promote solid learning.

Guided Practice

The author reviews practical guidelines for using these common forms of guided practice: homework, worksheets, and computer-based drill and practice.

Inquiry

Inquiry examines the three elements of inquiry: intriguing investigations, student discourse, and thoughtful reflection. Discussions of teacher behavior emphasize techniques to promote the most effective learning.

Instructional Technology—Independent Learning

This chapter focuses what to look for when searching out and evaluating interactive multimedia software that can support a desired type of learning.

Lecture

Lectures are a common teaching strategy. This chapter examines when it is and is not appropriate, how to prepare a lecture, and how to incorporate activities. It offers suggestions to keep lectures stimulating and reviews the use of visuals and questions and answers.

Memorization

This chapter examines the place of memorization in the learning experience. It emphasizes use of mnemonic devices and describes numerous examples and presents general tips on using memory systems.

Note-taking/Graphic Organizers

Note-taking/Graphic Organizers provides note-taking tips and strategies and considers how to choose the best graphic organizers for particular types of information and learning experiences. A variety of organizers are examined with examples provided.

Presentation/Exhibitions

This chapter shares multiple strategies for designing successful presentations and discusses how students can use exhibitions to demonstrate learning.

Problem-based Learning

This chapter emphasizes how a problem-based learning strategy must begin with real-world problems. It diagrams the learning cycle that comes into play and overviews the teacher's role in facilitating the exercise.

Project Design

Project Design examines designing a project as a simpler four-step-process suitable for younger students and a more advanced eight-step-process that demonstrates that solutions can introduce more problems.

Research

This chapter describes four types of research—scientific, social, analytical, and descriptive—and defines the steps in each. It provides suggestions for using the Internet and proper methods for citing sources. It then gives ideas for teaching students to use the library and to choose effective topics.

Simulation/Role-playing

Simulation/role-playing is a versatile strategy that can be used for presentations, guidance, practice, and assessment. Examples are given. Methods for designing and implementing them are provided.

Socratic Seminar

The Socratic seminar consists of four independent elements: the text, questions raised, the seminar leader, and the participants. This chapter describes the teacher's role as a facilitator and offers suggestions for preparing and conducting a seminar.

Teacher Questions

This chapter describes the different types of questions a teacher can use to prompt student learning and gives suggestions on how to construct and utilize them.

Work-based Learning

The final strategy provides examples of work-based learning strategies and describes the organizational structures involved in implementing a work-based program. Issues that should be considered when developing a program and methods for assessing the quality of the teaching and learning are presented.

 # Introduction

To the Teacher

Teaching is a craft practiced by skilled professionals, not an exact science in which any person can follow a standard recipe that guarantees success. Even the best teaching recommendations don't work in every situation for every student. Successful teachers not only teach well, but are also able to make good decisions about what strategies work in various situations. Successful teachers also learn through experience what works in various instructional activities.

Instead of relying solely on trial and error, this teacher handbook provides a resource for continuous improvement of your craft. The summary of instructional strategies helps you add to your professional "toolkit."

This resource also helps you analyze the variables in teaching situations and systematically select strategies that are likely to lead students to success. When you are comfortable and confident with several instructional strategies, you have choices in creating effective learning experiences. This gives you a much greater chance of presenting a lesson that reaches your students.

As you continue on your journey as a teacher, the suggestions in this handbook (as well as Volume 2) will help you to strengthen your professional repertoire and make good decisions about how to present material. Better decisions will lead to more motivated and engaged students. Those satisfying moments when everything works well in teaching are why most teachers joined the profession. Use the ideas in this handbook to increase your effectiveness with students.

Several important concepts are presented in this Introduction that apply to all instructional strategies. The first is the Rigor/Relevance Framework®, a tool developed by the International Center for Leadership in

Education to measure the rigor and relevance of curriculum, instruction, and assessment. When you become familiar with the Framework, you will be able to use it to facilitate learning experiences for your students that are high in cognitive skill development and contain real-world applications.

Next comes the International Center's Performance Planning Model. The interrelationship of curriculum, instruction, and assessment will become more apparent to you as you explore the complex process of curriculum planning. As a part of this process, instructional strategies can motivate the learner to engage in more rigorous and relevant learning.

Using the Rigor/Relevance Framework®

The Rigor/Relevance Framework® is a tool developed by the International Center to examine curriculum, instruction, and assessment. It uses a familiar knowledge taxonomy, while encouraging a move to application of knowledge. The Rigor/Relevance Framework helps make explicit the relevance of learning to the real world, broadening the historically narrow focus on acquisition of knowledge.

The Rigor/Relevance Framework is based on two dimensions of higher standards and student achievement. One is a continuum of knowledge based on the six levels of Bloom's Taxonomy, which describes the increasingly complex ways in which we think. The low end is acquiring knowledge and being able to recall or locate that knowledge in a simple manner (acquisition level). Just as a computer conducts a word search in a word processing program, a competent person at this level can scan through thousands of bits of information in the brain to locate that desired knowledge.

Rigor/Relevance Framework®

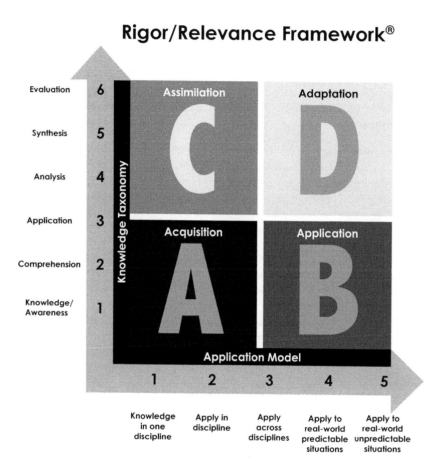

The high end of the knowledge continuum labels more complex ways in which we use knowledge. At this level, knowledge is fully integrated into our minds, and we can do much more than locate knowledge. We can take several pieces of knowledge and combine them in both logical and creative ways. Assimilation of knowledge is a good way to describe this high level of the thinking continuum. Assimilation is often referred to as a higher-order thinking skill. At this level, the student can find effective solutions to complex problems and create unique work.

The other continuum is one of action. While the knowledge continuum can be passive, the action continuum, based on the five levels of the Application Model, describes putting knowledge to use. At the low end (acquisition level), there is knowledge acquired for its own sake. At the high end of the continuum is using that knowledge to solve unpredictable problems, particularly from the real world, and to create projects, designs, and other works.

Together, the Knowledge Taxonomy and Application Model form the Rigor/Relevance Framework. A more extensive discussion of the Rigor/Relevance Framework can be found in *Using Rigor and Relevance to Create Effective Instruction*, published by the International Center. This handbook also includes activities for understanding how to use the Framework in planning curriculum and assessment.

The Rigor/Relevance Framework has four quadrants. Quadrant A represents simple recall and basic understanding of knowledge for its own sake. Directly above is Quadrant C, which represents more complex thinking, but still knowledge for its own sake. Examples of Quadrant A knowledge are knowing that the world is round and that Shakespeare wrote *Hamlet*. Quadrant C embraces higher levels of knowledge, such as knowing how the U.S. political system works and analyzing the benefits and challenges of the cultural diversity of this nation versus other nations.

Quadrants B and D represent action or high degrees of application. Quadrant B would include knowing how to use math skills to make purchases and count change. The ability to access information in wide-area network systems and gather knowledge from a variety of sources to solve a complex problem in the workplace is an example of Quadrant D knowledge.

These examples are skills in technical reading and writing.

Quadrant A: Define vocabulary terms needed to understand content of a classroom simulation.

Quadrant B: Complete a simulation following the directions given by the instructor.

Quadrant C: Compare and contrast the information gained from two simulations with that gained from reading a text on the same topic.

Quadrant D: Synthesize information from a range of sources (e.g., texts, media sources, simulations), presenting solutions to conflicting information.

Each of these four quadrants can be labeled with a term that characterizes the learning or student performance that occurs there.

Quadrant A — Acquisition

Students gather and store bits of knowledge and information. Students are primarily expected to remember or understand this acquired knowledge.

Quadrant B — Application

Students use acquired knowledge to solve problems, design solutions, and complete work. The highest level of application is to apply appropriate knowledge to new and unpredictable situations.

Quadrant C — Assimilation

Students extend and refine their knowledge so that they can use it automatically and routinely to analyze and solve problems and create solutions.

Quadrant D — Adaptation

Students have the competence to think in complex ways and also to apply knowledge and skills they have acquired. Even when confronted with perplexing unknowns, students are able to use their extensive knowledge base and skills to create unique solutions and take action that further develops their skills and knowledge.

In 2001 Bloom's Knowledge Taxonomy was updated and revised by Lorin Anderson, a student of Bloom's, and David Krathwohl, a colleague, to reflect the movement to standards-based curricula and assessment. Nouns in Bloom's original model were changed to verb forms (for example, *knowledge* to *remembering* and *comprehension* to *understanding*) and slightly reordered. We believe that the original Bloom's taxonomy as shown in our Rigor/Relevance Framework clearly describes expectations for Quadrants A, B, C, and D. The revised Bloom's elevates the importance of Quadrants B and D and indicates how 21st-century lessons should be built. We regard both the original and revised taxonomies as necessary and important.

The Rigor/Relevance Framework is easy to understand. With its simple, straightforward structure, it can serve as a bridge between school and the community. It offers a common language with which to express the notion of more rigorous and relevant standards and encompasses much of what parents, business leaders, and community members want students to learn.

The Framework is versatile; you can use it in the development of instruction and assessment. Likewise, you can use it to measure your progress in adding rigor and relevance to instruction and to select appropriate instructional strategies to meet learner needs and higher achievement goals.

Planning Instruction

To attain higher levels of rigor and relevance, instruction and assessment must not be separate and linear, but rather interrelated. Good learning takes place when there is a dynamic linkage of all components. In rigorous and relevant learning, instruction and assessment should have significant overlap. Authentic assessment should occur naturally as part of the instructional process. The current assessment reform movement seeks to place greater emphasis on student performance as opposed to simply recall of facts. Planning good instruction and assessment is easier if you abandon the image of linear progression of assessment following instruction.

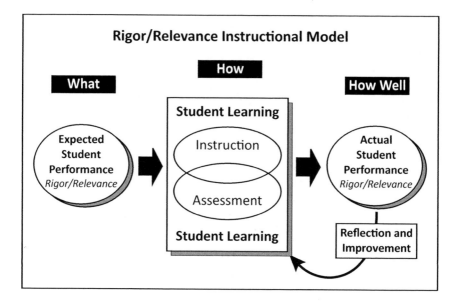

Curriculum planning occurs prior to instruction and assessment. Without effective planning, there is little likelihood that students will achieve the expected rigorous and relevant learning. Curriculum planning is a complex process. It is much more than picking out a work of literature or a textbook chapter and deciding that it would make a good instructional topic. Teacher experience and student data should be considered in order to make thoughtful decisions about instruction and assessment.

When teachers hear the word "curriculum," they generally think of unit or lesson plans that describe teaching procedures and/or student activities that would take place in a classroom. It is natural to think about these plans and immediately jump to imagine what they would look like in their classrooms. Teachers are under constant pressure to present activities that engage students, and there is little time to do much planning — such is the structure of the U.S. education system.

While curriculum must be organized into unit plans and lessons plans, curriculum planning does not begin with them. Teachers who begin and end their curriculum planning by writing a lesson plan miss important curriculum decisions.

The curriculum is a means to an end: a performance by the student. Teachers typically focus on a particular topic (e.g., volume of three-dimensional figures), use a particular resource (e.g., Periodic Table of Elements), and choose specific instructional methods (e.g., problem-based learning) to cause learning that meets a given standard. However, each of these decisions is actually a step in a learning process that should end in a performance by the student to demonstrate learning. Student activity without an end performance in mind is often busy work. Instruction, no matter how engaging or intellectual, is only beneficial if it ends with students demonstrating their knowledge and skills resulting from the learning experience. A performance approach to curriculum planning should begin with the specific student performance.

This backwards approach to curricular design also departs from another unfortunate but common practice: thinking about assessment as something to plan at the end, after teaching is completed. Rather than creating assessments near the conclusion of a unit of study (or relying on the tests provided by textbook publishers, which may not assess state standards completely or appropriately), backwards design calls for thinking about the work students will produce and how it might be assessed as you begin to plan a unit or course. Once you focus on a clear student performance, it is easier to select appropriate instructional strategies that will help students achieve that performance.

There are four major steps in planning rigorous and relevant instruction:

1. Define the focus of learning.
2. Create the student performance.
3. Design the assessment.
4. Develop the learning experiences.

The four steps are presented in the order in which ideal planning should occur. You select appropriate strategies in Step 4, after defining the focus, student performance, and assessment.

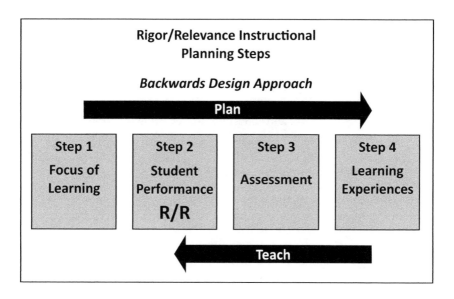

Selecting Strategies

The appropriateness of using any of the instructional strategies described in this handbook in individual situations depends upon matching the characteristics of the strategy, the learners, and what needs to be learned. All of these factors should be considered when selecting the best strategy for the learning situation. The more familiar you are with the strategies, the more likely you are to select the best strategy.

Although each strategy is described separately, the strategies are rarely used independently. When creating instructional units, you will typically select several strategies. For example, a lecture may precede a demonstration and ultimately lead to a problem-based exercise. Keeping in mind the strengths of each strategy will help you to create effective instructional experiences for your students.

Instructional Strategies and the Rigor/Relevance Framework

The first criterion to consider in selecting strategies is the level of student performance. When students are expected to demonstrate high levels of complex use of knowledge, then the instructional strategy used must give students experience with complex use of knowledge. In contrast, if students are only expected to recall knowledge, then the selected strategy can be simple, straightforward instruction. High levels of student performance often require application of knowledge.

Again, the instruction needs to match this level of expectation and give students learning experiences in which they apply knowledge.

The best way to develop a systematic approach to matching instructional strategy to the expected level of student performance is through the knowledge taxonomy and application model in the Rigor/Relevance Framework. The instructional strategies can be related to a particular quadrant of the Rigor/Relevance Framework. Likewise, the expected levels of student performance can be related to the Rigor/Relevance Framework. Select instructional strategies that work best for the quadrant in which your student objectives are located. When used at the right time, these strategies can help students to achieve expected standards. In the following chart, each strategy is rated as to its appropriateness for each of the four quadrants.

APPLICATION

A version of this graphic appears on the first page of the description of each strategy. The more stars in a quadrant of the Rigor/Relevance Framework, the more ideal the strategy is for teaching at that level.

Instructional Strategies and the Rigor/Relevance Framework

Strategy	Acquisition Quadrant A	Assimilation Quadrant C	Application Quadrant B	Adaptation Quadrant D
Brainstorming	★★	★★★	★	★★★
Cooperative Learning	★★	★★	★★★	★★★
Demonstration	★	★	★★★	★★
Guided Practice	★★★	★★	★★	★
Inquiry	★	★★★	★★	★★★
Instructional Technology— Independent Learning	★★	★★★	★★★	★★★
Lecture	★★★	★★	★	★
Memorization	★★★	★★	★★	★
Note-taking/Graphic Organizers	★★	★★	★★	★★
Presentations/Exhibitions	★	★★	★★	★★★
Problem-based Learning	★★	★★	★★★	★★★
Project Design	★	★	★★★	★★★
Research	★★	★★★	★	★★★
Simulation/Role-playing	★★	★★	★★★	★★★
Socratic Seminar	★	★★★	★	★★★
Teacher Questions	★★	★★★	★	★★★
Work-based Learning	★★	★★	★★★	★★★
Key ★★★ Ideal Strategy ★★ Appropriate Strategy ★ Least Appropriate Strategy				

Changing Roles

Strategy	Role of the Teacher	Role of the Student
Brainstorming	Cheerleader • Encourages participation • Is creative, has fun	Idea Generator • Thinks creatively • Makes new connections
Cooperative Learning	Parent • Prepares students in advance • Give students responsibility • Provides for equal participation	Peer Participant • Collaborates in learning process • Gives supportive feedback
Demonstration	Salesperson • Gives organized presentations • Has students replicate	Interested Observer • Watches carefully • Asks questions • Rehearses in his/her mind
Guided Practice	Coach • Sets practice rules • Ties learning goals to practice	Athlete at Practice • Remembers basic techniques • Repeats, repeats, repeats • Focuses on achievement
Inquiry	Mystery Writer • Leads to "discovery" • Provides clues • Foreshadows events	Scientist • Asks questions • Makes observations • Tests hypotheses
Instructional Technology— Independent Learning	Pilot • Integrates technology • Is knowledgeable about systems • Monitors learning systems	Explorer • Follows new paths to learning • Uses technology • Shares with others

Changing Roles

Strategy	Role of the Teacher	Role of the Student
Lecture	Expert • Directs thinking • Shares knowledge • Evaluates students	Listener • Pays attention • Relates to previous knowledge • Organizes knowledge
Memorization	Magician • Teaches "tricks of the trade" • Creates new tricks	Sorcerer's Apprentice • Copies traditional techniques • Experiments with new tricks
Note-taking/ Graphic Organizers	Master Mechanic • Knows right tool for the job • Provides important information • Teaches how to use the tools	Artisan • Captures ideas • Uses fundamental tools • Expresses personal creativity
Presentations/ Exhibitions	Olympic Judge • Establishes ideal performance • Evaluates students	Speaker • Shows well researched preparation • Has good platform skills • Informs the audience
Problem-based Learning	Coach • Presents problem situation • Encourages skill development • Supports students in the process	Detective • Analyzes the situation • Makes detailed observations • Seeks solutions
Project Design	Consultant • Provides background on project • Sets design specifications • Advises on process	Engineer • Examines the design specifications • Designs solutions • Tests solutions

Changing Roles

Strategy	Role of the Teacher	Role of the Student
Research	Resource Person • Teaches problem-solving • Poses problems • Translates into students' world	Scientist • Poses problems • Collects evidence • Organizes information
Simulation/ Role-playing	Stager • Manages the situation • Sets simulation/game in motion • Watches from the wings	Player • Focuses on the goal • Plays role with enthusiasm • Strives to improve
Socratic Seminar	Travel Agent • Enables learning from group • Guides group's journey	Journalist • Gathers and analyzes information • Organizes thoughts and ideas • Expresses ideas clearly
Teacher Questions	Conductor • Orchestrates learning • Guides performance	Expert • Responds to questions • Seeks new information
Work-based Learning	Navigator • Guides students • Shows students "destination" • Connects school and work	Apprentice • Models the master worker • Develops habits of the jobs • Seeks to improve constantly

Instructional Strategies and Learning Styles

One factor to consider in selecting instructional strategies is students' learning styles. Certain strategies are more effective with a particular learning style. When matched to students' learning styles, these strategies can help students achieve at higher levels. Four broad categories of learning styles are listed below.

Concrete-Sequential learners respond to well-organized instruction that requires them to recall and construct correct responses.

Abstract-Sequential learners respond to more collaborative instruction that requires them to analyze information and explain answers.

Concrete-Random learners respond to opportunities to be creative and design products and individual responses.

Abstract-Random learners respond to creative learning activities.

In the following chart, each strategy is rated as to its usefulness for each of the four learning styles.

Instructional Strategies and Learning Styles

Strategy	Concrete-Sequential	Abstract-Sequential	Concrete-Random	Abstract-Random
Brainstorming	★	★★	★★	★★★
Cooperative Learning	★	★★★	★★	★★
Demonstration	★★★	★★	★★	★
Guided Practice	★★★	★★	★★	★
Inquiry	★	★★	★★	★★★
Instructional Technology— Independent Learning	★★	★★	★★★	★★
Lecture	★★★	★★	★	★
Memorization	★★★	★	★★	★

Instructional Strategies and Learning Styles

Strategy	Concrete-Sequential	Abstract-Sequential	Concrete-Random	Abstract-Random
Note-taking/ Graphic Organizers	★ ★	★ ★	★ ★	★ ★
Presentations/ Exhibitions	★ ★	★ ★	★ ★	★ ★ ★
Problem-based Learning	★	★ ★ ★	★ ★ ★	★ ★
Project Design	★ ★	★	★ ★ ★	★
Research	★ ★	★ ★ ★	★ ★	★
Simulation/ Role-playing	★	★	★ ★	★ ★ ★
Socratic Seminar	★	★ ★ ★	★	★ ★
Teacher Questions	★ ★ ★	★ ★	★ ★	★
Work-based Learning	★ ★	★	★ ★ ★	★ ★

Key   ★ ★ ★ Ideal Strategy   ★ ★ Appropriate Strategy
★ Least Appropriate Strategy

Instructional Strategies and Assessment

Various types of assessments can be used to measure what a student knows and is able to do. Learning through a particular instructional strategy is best measured by an assessment type that parallels the strategy. Making a conscious effort to mirror instruction in assessment will enhance the student's ability to perform.

The following chart correlates the appropriateness of the instructional strategies to the eight most frequently used types of assessment.

Types of Assessment

- Multiple Choice
- Constructed Response
- Extended Response
- Process Performance
- Product Performance
- Portfolio
- Interview
- Self-reflection

Instructional Strategies and Assessment

Strategy	Multiple Choice	Constructed Response	Extended Response	Process Performance	Product Performance	Portfolio	Interview	Self-reflection
Brainstorming	★	★	★	★★★	★★	★★	★★	★★★
Cooperative Learning	★	★	★★	★★★	★★★	★★	★★	★★
Demonstration	★★	★★★	★★	★★★	★★	★★	★	★
Guided Practice	★★★	★★★	★★	★★★	★★	★★	★	★
Inquiry	★	★	★★	★★	★★★	★★	★★★	★★★
Instructional Technology— Independent Learning	★★	★	★	★★	★★★	★★★	★★	★★
Lecture	★★★	★★★	★★★	★	★	★	★★	★

Instructional Strategies and Assessment

Strategy	Multiple Choice	Constructed Response	Extended Response	Process Performance	Product Performance	Portfolio	Interview	Self-reflection
Memorization	★★★	★★★	★★	★★★	★★	★	★	★
Note-taking/ Graphic Organizers	★	★★	★★★	★	★★	★★	★★	★★★
Presentations/ Exhibitions	★	★	★★	★★★	★★★	★★★	★★	★★★
Problem-based Learning	★	★★	★★★	★★★	★★★	★★	★★	★★
Project Design	★	★★	★★★	★★★	★★★	★★★	★★	★★
Research	★	★	★★	★★★	★★★	★★★	★★	★★★
Simulation/ Role-playing	★	★	★★	★★★	★	★	★★	★★★
Socratic Seminar	★	★	★★★	★★	★	★	★★★	★★★
Teacher Questions	★★	★★★	★★	★	★	★	★★	★★
Work-based Learning	★	★	★★	★★★	★★★	★★★	★★★	★★

Key ★★★ Ideal Strategy ★★ Appropriate Strategy
★ Least Appropriate Strategy

Instructional Strategies and Educational Technology

A continuing debate centers on whether technology is the panacea that will help many students learn at higher levels or an exciting fad that is a temporary distraction from the real process of learning. The potential is there for either outcome. The degree to which technology has positive impacts on learning depends on the way it is applied in the classroom and beyond.

When used effectively, technology offers exciting possibilities for expanding learning beyond what schools have taught before. Technology accommodates various learning styles. Technology puts vast amounts of knowledge at students' fingertips. Information on every subject imaginable is available for study in all curriculum areas.

Technology offers students a chance to delve deeply into subjects. Greater accessibility to information gives students the opportunity to gather data easily and analyze and synthesize it in new ways. Students can manipulate data to identify those portions that are relevant to their needs. They can integrate data from one subject area to another and use the information to enhance their understanding.

Technology links curriculum with real-world experiences both inside and outside school. Using telecommunications and computer networks, students can work together in cooperative learning situations to help solve real problems, tying their education to real-life situations and giving them invaluable learning experiences.

Technology gives you a tool to create your own teaching materials, to go beyond required textbooks and use alternate resources, and to reorganize information in new ways. Students can also manipulate and reorder what they learn, giving them greater control over their learning.

Technology can enhance any of the instructional strategies. The following chart lists a few ways that education technology can be used with each of the strategies.

Instructional Strategies and Educational Technology

Strategy	Application of Technology
Brainstorming	• Students can use computers or mobile devices to record and display brainstormed ideas. • Word processing software is excellent for editing, sorting and organizing brainstormed lists.
Cooperative Learning	• Distribute discussion topics to students via computer or mobile devices. • Students can research topics via the Internet and software resources. • Students can record reflections on computer. • Students can illustrate group findings with computer graphic displays.
Demonstration	• Use digital media to show complex tasks that are too expensive or dangerous to do live. • Students can review previous demonstrations from computer files or via mobile devices or the Internet.
Guided Practice	• Students can use drill and practice software to reinforce fundamental skills. • Provide enhancing activities for students who learn at a faster pace.
Inquiry	• Pose initial questions and intriguing investigations on computer or mobile device. • Students can collaborate with other students and experts off-site via the Internet. • Students can record reflections on computer or mobile device.
Instructional Technology— Independent Learning	• Technology must be used to give students direct experience learning with multi-media.

Instructional Strategies and Educational Technology

Strategy	Application of Technology
Lecture	• Use computer visuals to illustrate lectures. • Record and make lectures available in podcast or video cast.
Memorization	• Students can practice mnemonics on computer or mobile device.
Note-taking/ Graphic Organizers	• Students can use word processing software for taking notes. • Make reference notes available for students on the Internet. • Graphic organizing software is excellent for creating graphical displays of information. • Distribute note-taking templates to students via networks.
Presentations/ Exhibitions	• Students can use multimedia software to create presentations. • Students can use the Internet and reference software to research topics. • Enhance presentations with student recorded video.
Problem-based Learning	• Pose problems on computers or mobile devices. • Students can use computer networks to research problems. • Students can use computer software for reference of decisions and expert systems. • Students can create and display solutions with visual software.

Instructional Strategies and Educational Technology

Strategy	Application of Technology
Project Design	• Students can create project designs and model solutions on computers or mobile devices. • Students can use calculators, mobile devices, and computers for calculating design data. • Students can use robots to conduct design tests. • Students can use the Internet to collect information on design needs.
Research	• Students can use the Internet and reference software to research topics.
Simulation/ Role-playing	• Students can use computer simulations. • Students can use education learning games for individual instruction.
Socratic Seminar	• Students can engage in discussion with students at remote locations through the Internet. • Students can use the Internet to research questions posed.
Teacher Questions	• Use software for brainstorming and keeping track of effective classroom questions.
Work-based Learning	• Students can use computer software as it is used in the workplace.

APPLICATION

Brainstorming

Rules for Brainstorming

Before beginning the brainstorming process, students need to be reminded of the rules (listed below). Sometimes, it may be necessary during the actual brainstorming session to remind students of these rules.

- **No critical remarks are allowed.** Judgment on all ideas is deferred. No one may evaluate or criticize anything that anyone else says. Accept all suggestions even if they seem very farfetched.

- **"Hitchhiking" is okay.** Adding to or modifying another person's idea is fine. The idea may be adapted, combined, magnified, minimized, rearranged, substituted, changed, or improved. Let alternatives prompt additional alternatives. The more thinking, the better.

- **"Free-wheeling" is welcomed.** The wilder the ideas, the better. No one should hold back any thoughts. Sometimes it takes a crazy or far-out idea to prompt a useful one.

- **Quantity is desired.** The more ideas, the better. Typically, only a small percentage of ideas from a brainstorming session are usable. Thus, the more ideas to begin with, the greater the potential for more winning solutions. From quantity will come quality.

- **Silence is fine.** It is all right to have lulls in the idea generation. During periods of silence, students are usually thinking. Let the silence linger until ideas pop up.

- **A time limit is necessary.** Stick to a set time limit. Five to ten minutes, depending on the question, is usually ample time to generate sufficient ideas. A time limit creates a sense of urgency and helps to keep ideas flowing.

- **Evaluation comes later.** Don't be fussy. Students should not be worrying about any sort of correctness or appropriateness of ideas. Hold off any type of evaluation until after the brainstorming session.

When to Use Brainstorming

When you introduce new material, brainstorming is a technique that helps you involve all students. You can use this technique to begin a discussion at any time on any topic; the ideas can then be further refined. If you want to stimulate your students' thinking, engage them in brainstorming.

In addition to generating ideas, brainstorming can be used:

1. To help solve a problem.
2. To find out what students already know about a topic.
3. To turn individual ideas into group ideas.
4. To provide material for goal setting.
5. As a needs assessment technique.
6. To get talkative students to listen.
7. To get quieter students to speak up.
8. To evaluate an activity.

9. To set the stage for the formation of subgroups to carry out the ideas.

10. To add life to what may be an otherwise dull introductory lecture.

11. As an icebreaker at the beginning of a semester.

Guidelines for Effective Brainstorming

As the facilitator of the brainstorming session, you need to ensure that the idea generation is structured, even though the brainstorming session appears to be freewheeling. Both you and your students should become familiar with the rules for effective brainstorming. Here are some general suggestions and some ideas for rules to establish.

- Present a well-defined, clear problem.
- Assign someone the task of recording all ideas as they are given.
- You can call out an idea without being recognized.
- Give only one idea at a time.
- Be brief; it is not necessary to explain, elaborate, or justify your ideas.
- Record all ideas where everyone can see them as they are presented.
- Since this is a group exercise, there should be at least four students in the exercise.
- Keep your mind open to all ideas.
- Do not belittle any ideas; suspend judgment.
- Watch for body language or facial expressions that demonstrate evaluation of ideas.
- Build on the thoughts of others.
- Encourage way-out and odd ideas.
- Have a student timekeeper to keep the group focused and tell when time is up.

- Once time is up or all ideas are exhausted, begin evaluating which ideas are possibilities and which ones need to be discarded.

- After sorting through ideas, try to come up with a manageable number of solutions, perhaps three to five. Mixing and matching ideas to form new ones is a common part of the sorting process.

- Throughout the entire session, encourage all students to participate and ensure that everyone's thoughts are treated with respect.

- Have a student rule-keeper to help enforce these guidelines.

Sometimes students will just not be in a creative mood, or the well of ideas will run dry very early in the session and students may become bored with the process. When that occurs, other types of brainstorming activities may help get the group back in a participatory mood. Here are several examples.

In **trigger** sessions, students generate ideas independently and silently and then read them aloud to the other students, who are encouraged to build on the ideas given. In **recorded round robin**, each student is given a card with the problem and instructions to add a new idea. The card then is passed from one student to another who continues to add an idea that is prompted by the ideas on the card. Cards may be passed several times among students. During a **wildest idea** session, students give the most far-out ideas imaginable. Other students use these to come up with additional new ideas.

In some cases, **environmental changes** can spark renewed creativity. For example, replace the facilitator or recorder; change to a new color of pen being used for recording; rearrange students so that they are in a different seating arrangement; have everyone stand and take a stretch break; move the flip-chart to another place in the room. The facilitator may have to work at encouraging participation.

If a question draws hardly any responses, go back to ensure that students fully understand the problem and/or the brainstorming process.

Sample Brainstorming Ideas

Ideas for brainstorming sessions can come from individual disciplines, across disciplines, background knowledge, or experience. At the primary or early elementary level, students might be asked to brainstorm words that rhyme with *kind*, questions to ask a storybook character, ways to use numbers, uses of a telephone. In a secondary integrated math/science/technology course, students might brainstorm mathematical formulas used in construction work, tools needed to repair household items, factors having a negative impact on the environment. There are myriad topics and problems conducive to brainstorming sessions.

Brainstorming Variations

A number of variations on brainstorming have been developed that you may find useful, depending on the problem to be solved, the group makeup, and the amount of time to be devoted to generating ideas. When selecting a form of brainstorming, be sure to correlate the technique with your desired end result. Variations on brainstorming include the following:

Reverse Approach. In a typical brainstorming session, the goal is to generate positive things: new ideas, solutions, uses, etc. Using the reverse approach, the problem is approached in a negative way. The objective is to make things right by first identifying the things that are wrong. Have students brainstorm deficiencies and then brainstorm ways to overcome these.

For example, suppose the problem to solve concerns how to improve poor attendance rate at school. Brainstorming ways to increase absenteeism and class cutting can stimulate new thinking on the issue. Some possible answers might be: no consequences for not attending school/class; make instruction more boring; eliminate the guidance department; discontinue the attendance policy; make no parent contacts, etc. From these thoughts, ideas to improve the situation easily flow.

SIL Method. SIL is an acronym for the German words for "Successive Integration of Problem Elements." In this method, all ideas may not be necessarily used, but they are heard and tried out.

1. Idea generation is done individually in writing.
2. Two group members read their written ideas aloud.
3. The other group members listen and attempt to integrate the ideas into one solution.
4. A third student reads his/her idea.
5. The rest of the class integrates the third idea with the solution found from the first two students' thoughts.
6. This process continues until all ideas are entertained.

Pause That Refreshes. Brainstorming involves rapid idea generation by students and continued encouragement by the teacher or facilitator of the session to give even more ideas. Variations of this procedure involve stopping idea generation for a silent period, a time for renewal, and then returning to the idea-giving stage.

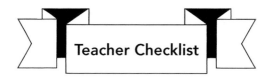

Teacher Checklist

Yes   No

☐   ☐   The problem was clear and well defined for students.

☐   ☐   The rules for brainstorming were explained to and understood by students.

☐   ☐   The strategy was appropriate for generation of ideas for the topic given.

☐   ☐   All ideas were accepted and recorded.

☐   ☐   All students gave at least one idea.

☐   ☐   Students' remarks stimulated other ideas in a chain reaction effect.

☐   ☐   Students demonstrated creative thinking.

☐   ☐   All students were encouraged to participate.

☐   ☐   An appropriate pace and time limit were followed.

☐   ☐   If rules were broken, they were enforced with explanation.

☐   ☐   Praise was used to keep ideas flowing.

☐   ☐   Students were complimented on their cooperation and productivity.

☐   ☐   At the start of the evaluation process, ideas were clarified for students.

☐   ☐   Students agreed on which ideas to eliminate, join with other ideas, rephrase, consider as real possibilities, etc.

Yes	No	
☐	☐	Everyone's input was treated with respect.
☐	☐	Students arrived at a few good solutions/ideas from the list.
☐	☐	Where implementation of ideas was appropriate, the ideas were put into action and students discussed the results.

APPLICATION

Cooperative Learning

Basic Elements of Cooperative Learning

According to Johnson and Johnson (*Circles of Learning*, 1986), there are five essential components of any cooperative learning model or method.

1. **Positive Interdependence.** Students must feel that they need one another in order to succeed, that they will "sink or swim" together. It takes everyone to complete the task. When students perceive that their achievement is correlated with that of other students, they experience positive interdependence. Students recognize that each member functions as a part of a team and that the success of the whole group depends on the contributions of each member. This relationship fosters peer tutoring, support, and encouragement. Some ways to create this feeling are to:

- establish mutual goals; students must learn a given material and make sure that all other members learn it as well.

- give joint rewards; group members receive individual bonus points if all members score above a given percentage on a test.

- provide a task structure that involves a division of labor.

- provide shared materials and information; for example, the group task is completed on a single sheet of paper or each member has only part of the information or materials necessary to complete an assignment.

- assign roles: time manager, encourager, classifier, summarizer, etc.

2. **Face-to-Face Interaction.** When students interact with other students orally and in writing, in pairs or small group activities, it maximizes student involvement and aids in concept development. Verbal exchanges, such as giving and receiving explanations, summarizing, debating, and elaborating, provide students the language needed to internalize information and exercise higher level thinking skills. For interaction to be productive and equalized, students must learn communication skills and key vocabulary.

3. **Individual Accountability.** Cooperative learning groups are successful to the extent that they promote individual as well as group effort and achievement. Thus, it is important to assess individual learning frequently so that group members can appropriately support and help each other. Monitoring each student's contribution deters any team member from becoming a "free rider" or a "workhorse." Some ways of structuring individual accountability include giving individual exams, assigning a minitopic per student, and having students initial their contributions to a team worksheet or project.

4. **Interpersonal and Small Group Skills.** Most students need to learn the social skills necessary to collaborate effectively with others in producing a common product or achieving a mutual goal. Therefore, skills such as active listening, group decisionmaking, leadership, and conflict management need to be taught to achieve effective group functioning.

5. **Group Processing.** Students need time and procedures to analyze how well their group is functioning. Individual students (self-evaluation), team members, student observers, or the teacher, can provide feedback. An integral part of feedback is group processing to analyze the effectiveness of the team. Social interaction skills are most needed when the cooperative task is more complex and less structured.

Cooperative Learning Instructional Methods

Practical classroom applications of cooperative learning principles have been developed by several independent groups of researchers. Their methods are aimed at reducing student isolation and individual competition and at increasing students' abilities to interact and work together toward common goals. The most commonly used cooperative learning structures are listed.

Student-Teams-Achievement Divisions (STAD) (Robert Slavin)

Whole Class: You present a lesson to the class.

Teams: Students assemble in teams of four or five members and complete activities to ensure that all members understand the lesson.

Individuals: Individuals take a quiz on the material. The team's overall score is determined by the extent to which each student improved over his/her past performance.

Teams-Games Tournament (TGT) (Robert Slavin)

The procedure in TGT is the same as STAD. However, members from each team vie in ability-grouped academic games. Each student earns points for the team according to his/her improvement over past performance. Team scores are usually posted.

Jigsaw (E. Aronson)

Teams: Students meet in teams of five.

Home Teams: Academic material is broken down into sections. You give each student an item of information that the student must teach to his/her teammates.

Expert Groups: Team members learn information from one another.

Home Teams: Experts return to home teams to share their expertise on the topic.

Individuals: Students may be tested individually for their mastery of the material.

Jigsaw II (Robert Slavin)

Jigsaw II is a modification of Jigsaw. In Jigsaw II, students obtain their information from textbooks, the Internet, narrative material, biographies, etc. Students discuss their topics in expert groups and teach their teammates what they have learned. Finally, students take a quiz on the material, and the scores are used to form individual and team scores.

Learning Together (Johnson and Johnson)

This method is closest to pure cooperation. After you have presented a lesson, students work together in small groups to complete an assignment or worksheet. The team as a whole receives praise and recognition for work completed.

Group Investigation (Sharan and Sharan)

This is the most complex method of cooperative learning. Students in small groups take substantial responsibility for deciding what they will learn, how they will organize themselves to learn it, and how they will communicate what they have learned to their classmates. Students are graded on the quality of the group's report to the class.

Think-Pair-Share (Kagan)

Individual: You pose a question; students work individually.

Team (Pair): Students pair up and share responses with one another; sometimes the pairs work to reach consensus.

Whole Class: Pairs share with class.

Numbered Heads Together (Kagan)

Teams generate a number of ideas; then each member chooses one to report to the class. All students stand. You call on one student to share and then sit down; any student(s) having a similar idea also sits.

Roundtable (Kagan)

You ask a question with many possible answers. The students will respond on one piece of paper. Each student writes one answer and then passes the paper to the person on his/her left. The response paper literally goes round the table.

Roundrobin (Kagan)

This is the oral counterpart of roundtable. Students take turns stating answers without recording them.

Three-Step Interview (Kagan)

You generate a topic. Students are grouped into pairs. One student becomes the interviewer, and the second student becomes the interviewee. Each student plays both roles on the given topic. Students complete a round-robin exercise where each student shares with the other team members what he/she learned in the interview.

Lineup (Kagan)

Team members divide and learn new information. Then they teach each other their part/topic.

Your Role

Successful cooperative learning requires you to train students to work together using clear procedures. Helping, sharing, and cooperating are classroom norms.

In the cooperative learning classroom you are not the sole expert who dictates instructions. You must be able to allow the students to make some choices as to the substance and goals of their learning activity.

Students participate actively in the process of acquiring knowledge as you facilitate the learning opportunities. Cooperative small groups shift instruction and supervision from direct to indirect. Authority becomes delegated through norms and roles. Considerable planning is required to create effective cooperative learning.

Your Responsibilities

1. **Decisions**

   Various decisions have to be made regarding the cooperative learning methods, size of group, assignment of students, arrangement of the classroom, instructional materials, and assignment of roles.

   The learning task will determine to a great extent the cooperative learning method you select. The room arrangement will also be determined by the cooperative learning method. Grouping, of course, requires changing the traditional room arrangement.

Other factors to consider when setting up the room include: what the groups will be doing, how visible groups need to be to one another, access to materials, etc. Materials make tasks more interesting. Using a variety will improve student motivation and interest.

When assigning roles, you need to be sensitive to students' strengths and weaknesses. Roles should assist in enforcing group norms. Roles should be rotated for different activities so that students can learn what each role involves.

Group composition is optimal at four to five for short-range projects. Larger groups may be used for longer-range projects provided subgroups or task forces within the larger group are established. You should assign students to groups. Groups should be heterogeneously mixed as to academic achievement, sex, race and ethnicity. Self-selection should only be done on the basis of interest in a particular topic. You should periodically change group composition, such as with a change in task.

2. **Setting Task and Positive Interdependence**

You need to explain the task, the criteria for success, and the desired student behaviors. Also, positive goal interdependence, individual accountability, and intergroup cooperation must be structured.

Introduce the task. Point out and discuss the different skills needed to complete the task. Discuss what each group will be doing, what each student will be responsible for, how the product/process will be presented, and how students will be evaluated. Develop group worksheets that students may work on together to reinforce content and skills. Prepare written instructions on the task and how to accomplish it. Expectations should be clear. Check instructions by working through them yourself, or have another teacher read them for sense and clarity. Set norms and roles that will require students to use one another as resources.

Cooperative norms for behavior should ensure that everyone:

- listens to one another
- contributes
- asks for help when needed
- helps others when asked

To ensure that each group member is accountable:

- Design worksheets to be completed by individuals but worked on by the group as a whole.
- Test students individually on content covered in the small group after the group task is completed.
- Structure the group so that each student is responsible for a specific part of the task.

3. Monitoring and Intervening

As facilitator, you need to intervene where necessary to provide task assistance and to monitor student behavior. Although the students are the "active" learners in cooperative learning, you need to introduce, guide, intervene, and close the lesson. Check and monitor the working groups but do not direct them. You are responsible to structure the learning activity and ensure that its implementation will result in student learning and achievement.

4. Evaluating and Processing

During group work, you should provide specific feedback on content and group process. Ask questions that reflect and extend experiences. Some categories for observation during group work are explaining concepts, encouraging participation, checking understanding, and organizing the work. By using norms and roles, constructive feedback processes can be built into group work. Use wrap-up sessions for students to share ideas, present products, and discuss their experiences working cooperatively.

Individual Student Responsibilities

1. Trying—improvement counts
2. Asking—requesting help, clarification from teammates
3. Helping—teammates, classmates, the teacher
4. Courtesy—requests, praisers, encouragers, no put downs
5. Filling roles:
   - Checker (checking for understanding and agreement)
   - Praiser/Encourager (praising effort, ideas, helping roles)
   - Recorder (recording ideas, decisions, processing, products)
   - Taskmaster (bringing the group back to the task)
   - Gatekeeper (ensuring all participate, no bully, no loafer)
   - Gofer (getting materials, books, etc.)
   - Reporter (sharing with other teams, class, teacher)

Team Responsibilities

1. Solving their own problems
2. Team questions only
3. Consulting with other teams and the teacher
4. Helping teammates, other teams, the teacher (if asked)
5. Listening

Two Rules for Students When Functioning in Groups

1. You are responsible for your own work and behavior.
2. You must be willing to help any group member who asks.

References

Aronson, E. *The Jigsaw Classroom.* Beverly Hills, CA: Sage Publications, 1978.

Johnson, D.W., and Johnson, R. *Learning Together and Alone: Cooperative, Competitive, and Individualist Learning.* Englewood Cliffs, NJ: Prentice-Hall, 1986.

Johnson, D.W., and Johnson, R. *Creative Conflict.* Edina, MN: Interaction Book Company, 1987.

Johnson, D.W., Johnson, R., and Holubec, E. *Circles of Learning: Cooperation in the Classroom*, 3rd Edition. Edina, MN: Interaction Book Company, 1990.

Kagan, S. *Cooperative Learning: Resources for Teachers.* San Clemente, CA: Kagan Publishing and Professional Development, 1994. www.KaganOnline.com

Sharan, S., and Sharan, Y. *Small-Group Teaching.* Englewood Cliffs, NJ: Technology Publications, 1976.

Slavin, R.E. *Cooperative Learning: Theory, Research, and Practice.* Englewood Cliffs, NJ: Prentice-Hall, 1990.

Slavin, R.E. *Student Team Learning: A Practical Guide to Cooperative Learning.* Washington, D.C.: National Education Association, 1991.

Teacher Checklist

Yes	No	
☐	☐	Students received training in norms and roles for cooperative learning.
☐	☐	Roles were assigned based on students' strengths and weaknesses.
☐	☐	The groups were heterogeneous.
☐	☐	The group size was appropriate for the task.
☐	☐	The room was arranged to ensure effective group functioning.
☐	☐	The cooperative learning method was compatible with the learning task.
☐	☐	The cooperative learning method was understood by students.
☐	☐	Materials needed for each group were easily accessible.
☐	☐	You and the students knew specifically what was to be learned.
☐	☐	Students understood the task.
☐	☐	Students understood positive interdependence in relation to the task.
☐	☐	Students understood what they were individually accountable for.
☐	☐	The criteria for success were clear and understood.

Yes	No	
☐	☐	Students understood what specific behaviors were expected.
☐	☐	Feedback was provided to groups through your questions and comments.
☐	☐	Students exhibited high levels of engagement.
☐	☐	Students gave and received peer feedback.
☐	☐	A wrap-up session gave students an opportunity to assess the team's success in group processing skills and in completion of the task.
☐	☐	Outcomes were evaluated in terms of task achievement, group functioning, and individual student performance or improvement.

APPLICATION

Demonstration

Definition of Demonstrations

Demonstrations are live visual exhibitions of a process or experiment. They can be used to show students correct techniques for operating equipment, set up experimentation, emphasize safety precautions, or introduce important concepts. Demonstrations use the power of visual learning. Many skills and concepts can be taught more effectively with a dramatic visual demonstration.

Demonstrations help students share learning experiences, through the interplay of ideas, observations, questions and comments on what they have observed. Demonstrations can add considerable interest to a lesson and make learning easier. The visual aspect of a demonstration helps students to remember.

Demonstrations are not as effective a learning technique as having students participate directly in a hands-on experiment of their own. However, demonstrations are the best strategy to reduce hazards, such as showing safety procedures or a process for handling dangerous materials. In this type of demonstration, the students observe only, and don't repeat the actions themselves.

A demonstration allows the teacher to model proper behavior. The teacher sets the standards of speed or accuracy that students are expected to follow after sufficient practice. Demonstrations can also reduce the time the students need to practice and reduce the likelihood of trial and error learning.

As with other teaching techniques, planning is essential to be sure that the demonstration will have maximum benefit in helping students learn. Effective demonstrations require the teacher to be competent at the skill — but not necessarily a world expert! If the teacher is unfamiliar with a skill, he/she should practice it prior to demonstrating it to a class of students. The teacher must be able to present the skill in easy, learnable steps or stages. The steps should lead to competence when practiced by students.

A demonstration should:

- capture students' interest
- draw on the personal ideas and experiences of the students
- create in students a desire to do the procedure
- make students think about what the demonstrator is doing and why it is done in that way
- provide an easy transition from observing to doing it in practice
- set standards — provide a "mental template" or good example to follow
- be followed by student application or replication of the skill

Steps in Preparation of a Demonstration

1. Analyze the skill or process to be taught.
2. Divide the activity into a series of steps and select key stages as teaching points.
3. Identify what may be difficult, unfamiliar, or confusing for a learner, as well as parts that may need more explanation or practice than others.

4. Prepare demonstration notes.

5. Assemble materials and prepare the physical setting.

6. Set up the demonstration area so that everyone will be able to see.

7. Prepare any handouts or visuals aids.

Steps in Giving a Demonstration

1. Explain the purpose of the demonstration.

2. Check what students already know about this skill or concept.

3. Point out any new or unusual features of the equipment or materials to be used.

4. Describe the process.

5. Review key steps or difficult parts.

6. Demonstrate the skill or process to present a "mental template" of a correct or appropriate performance.

7. Point out particular highlights as they occur, but don't talk the whole way through the demonstration.

8. Repeat specific parts afterwards, using slow or exaggerated movements if necessary.

9. Introduce essential information at suitable times, stressing main points and safety aspects.

10. Use visual aids if and when required.

11. Put away equipment and materials after use to set a good example for work habits.

12. Prepare the students to practice what they have observed.

Suggestions

- Display or have a handout of a list of key steps to reinforce these points with students.

- Encourage questions and ask the students questions to test their understanding of the process and steps.

- Ask one student to replicate the demonstration while others observe and comment. This approach lets you check any errors as they occur and provide further explanations if needed.

- Check the group's understanding of the key stages as the task is repeated.

- Don't demonstrate the incorrect method as the visual impact may remain with the students and confuse them. Explain things that can go wrong, but don't give a visual demonstration of them!

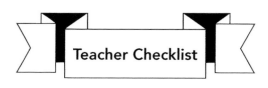

Teacher Checklist

Yes   No

☐   ☐   The demonstration was carefully divided into clear steps.

☐   ☐   The demonstration area was set up so that all class members could see.

☐   ☐   All necessary materials and equipment were assembled and prepared so that the demonstration flowed smoothly without distractions or interruptions.

☐   ☐   The demonstration was introduced by linking it to prior student knowledge.

☐   ☐   The importance of the demonstration was explained and an attempt was made to create interest.

☐   ☐   The key steps in the demonstration were explained and it was clear what students should expect to observe.

☐   ☐   The demonstration set a model of correct performance, including safety and proper procedures.

☐   ☐   Any special or difficult aspects were given extra attention or explanation.

☐   ☐   Follow-up activities were used to check that students understood the main steps.

☐   ☐   Students were provided opportunities for practice following the demonstration.

☐   ☐   Students were given feedback on their ability to replicate the demonstration.

APPLICATION

Guided Practice

This chapter reviews practical guidelines for using common forms of guided practice: homework, worksheets, and computer-based drill and practice.

Homework

The following list of "Tips for Effective Homework" comes from *Helping Your Students With Homework: A Guide for Teachers,* published by the U.S. Department of Education.

1. *Lay out expectations early in the school year.* Before handing out the first homework assignment, go over the ground rules. A written explanation of the homework expectations increases chances that assignments will be completed successfully. Write notes home laying out expectations, which parents or caregivers are asked to read, initial, and return. Talk with parents about homework at back-to-school night; telephone parents. Making special efforts to communicate with those who are hardest to reach.

2. *Create assignments with a purpose.* Some homework is **not** better than no homework at all. The quality of an assignment makes a huge difference in whether it gets done. Busywork is not an effective instructional strategy.

3. *Make sure students understand the purpose.* Most students appreciate understanding the purpose of an assignment, even if the purpose may not become evident until they are part way through an assignment or have completed it altogether.

4. *Make assignments focused and clear.* Focused assignments are easier for students to understand and complete. Homework that tries to introduce or reinforce too many ideas is less likely to contribute to learning. This is particularly true for students whose abstract thinking hasn't developed to the point where they can integrate many concepts successfully.

5. *Create assignments that challenge students to think.* Homework can give students an opportunity to apply a concept beyond the controlled conditions of the classroom. It can also help students pull together and connect information from different places, sources, and subjects. Good assignments often challenge students to break free of their usual way of thinking. Such assignments might require students to combine two ideas that are usually not associated.

6. *Vary assignments.* Students get bored if all assignments are similar. Try mixing approaches and styles. Since it's almost impossible for all assignments to interest all students, this approach increases the chances that all students will have some homework that they enjoy.

7. *Give homework that makes learning personal.* The assignments that work best relate to the students — the assignments are personal to them. These assignments allow students to draw upon their family, cultural, and community experiences and make learning relevant.

8. *Tie assignments to the present.* Students often complain that they can't relate to assignments involving events that took place in the distant past.

9. *Match assignments to the skills, interests, and needs of students.* Students are more apt to complete homework when assignments

are neither too easy nor too hard, match the students' preferred learning styles, and allow students to work on material that they truly enjoy. Provide assignments to a heterogeneous class of students that vary in style, format, and content. This assures that all students have some that suits them.

10. *Use school and community resources.* Many creative and rewarding homework assignments draw upon resources that are close at hand.

11. *Match assignments to your style of teaching.* Assignments are more apt to succeed if you are comfortable with them.

12. *Assign an appropriate amount of homework.* Many educators believe that homework is most effective for children in first through third grades when it does not exceed 20 minutes each school day. From fourth through sixth grades, many educators recommend from 20 to 40 minutes a school day for most students. For students in seventh through ninth grades, generally, up to 2 hours a school day is suitable. Ninety minutes to 2-½ hours per night are appropriate for grades 10 through 12. Amounts that vary from these guidelines are fine for some students.

13. *Encourage and teach good study habits.* Children need good study skills in order to complete assignments and gain the most from them academically. Unfortunately, many students haven't developed these skills, even by high school.

14. *Provide constructive feedback.* Students are more apt to do assignments and advance their learning when they get consistent and constructive feedback. Students need to know where they excelled and where they need to do more work on an assignment. This conveys the vital message that homework helps students learn and is important.

15. *Give praise and motivate.* Adults and children alike respond to praise. "Good first draft of your book report!" or "You've done a great job" can go a long way toward motivating students to complete assignments. Praise must be genuine. Children recognize insincere compliments.

16. *Give help as needed.* Students who don't understand an assignment need to know that help is available from you or another

appropriate person. Students at risk of academic failure or with personal difficulties may need extra support with both academic and logistical aspects of homework. It is important that they know it is okay to ask for help. In fact, it is imperative that they do so.

17. *Communicate with parents.* Student learning improves when you communicate with parents on a broad range of issues. Among the most vital of these is homework. Parents are not expected to know or teach specific information to their children, particularly as students get older. Parents can be an enormous help, however, in creating an environment at home that allows learning to take place. You can also help create situations that allow parents and educators to work together to strengthen all learning, including what takes place at home.

18. *Show respect for students.* Students are more inclined to complete assignments when you and the students respect one another. Students sense when teachers care about them and want them to do their best work.

Homework Guidelines

1. Set the expectations for homework early in the school year.

2. Don't give homework as punishment.

3. Don't give spur-of-the-moment homework assignments, especially if you expect students to devote their time and care to the work.

4. Don't assume because no questions are asked when you give the assignment that students have no questions about their homework.

5. Explain the purpose of every assignment.

6. Acknowledge and praise students' efforts to complete homework.

7. Listen to what students say about their experiences with homework.

8. Include parents by making your homework expectations clear and encouraging students to ask their parents for appropriate help.

9. Offer to help students before and after school with homework. You are the best judge about which assignments really must be completed independently.

10. Don't confuse excuses for incomplete homework assignments with legitimate reasons.

11. Make every effort to acknowledge completed homework assignments and, if you grade them, do so and return them right away.

12. Be consistent in the amount of time students are expected to devote to homework. Avoid assignments that are significantly larger than typical assignments.

Worksheets

In elementary school (and to a lesser extent in middle and high school) worksheets can help children develop good work habits and attitudes. Worksheets can:

- teach children the fundamentals of working independently
- encourage self-discipline and responsibility, as assignments provide youngsters the chance to manage time and meet deadlines

Worksheet assignments should have a clear purpose and be tied directly to the overall instructional plan. Like homework, worksheets should not be used as punishment. Students need to know the purpose of the worksheets and not consider them busy work. Worksheets require a fair amount of planning and thought as to why you are assigning them in the first place.

Worksheets can be used for practice of a procedure, vocabulary, application of concepts, or recall of information. Worksheets are also useful for independent research or observation. Worksheets used in this manner provide a good structure for students learning in individual learning centers. The worksheets provide students with questions to follow and become an easy tool on which to record their work for your review.

Computer- or Mobile Device-Based Drill and Practice

By its nature, computer-based and mobile device-based practice is a highly repetitive activity that, if not carefully crafted, can quickly lose learner interest. Students mechanically work through drill questions, pressing keys and moving on, with little real engagement of creative or critical thinking. In short, students can become bored, and the educational opportunity of the drill-and-practice exercise will be lost.

Variety in design and delivery is the key weapon in the war against boredom. Too often software developers attempt a "quick fix" of cute sounds and graphics, which signal the correctness or incorrectness of responses but add no real training value to the process. Too much "cuteness" can actually detract from, rather than enhance, the training goals.

Better alternatives exist to combat learner boredom. Whether you are reviewing software for purchase or designing your own computer drill-and-practice activities, consider the tips listed below.

- Employ a Short, Modular Approach

  Short guided practice segments are better than confronting the learner with a long list of repetitive questions that cover a broad spectrum of topics. Each segment should consist of a limited number of questions targeting very specific topics. (This is especially useful if exercises are integrated into a larger tutorial project.)

- Record the Learner's Exit Point

  Quite often students will use a guided practice tool on a number of occasions over a period of time. In these situations, learners find it both distracting and discouraging to be forced to "rework" materials covered in previous sessions. To avoid this problem, exercises should track learner use for quick navigation over "completed" sections of instruction.

- Interchange Questions and Responses

  One of the simplest ways to add variety to drill-and-practice questions, especially in multiple-choice questions is through the interchange of the question and response. The response becomes the key element in the new question stem and vice versa.

- Reorder Questions within an Exercise

  If learners will use a drill-and-practice tool more than once, the same questions should not always be presented in the same order. For maximum variety, it is best to have a large pool of questions — in equivalent form and level of difficulty — and randomly generate a "new" order each time the student begins the lesson.

- Student Responses

  After presenting the learner with a question (and possibly a number of alternative answers), the exercise waits for some form of student input in response. It could be multiple choice or some form of constructed response. The form of the question will determine both how the computer or mobile device receives and evaluates this input. Be sure to provide the student with clear instructions in how the input procedure works.

- Reinforcing Correct Answers

  Providing feedback for learner responses to drill-and-practice questions demands more than simple correct or incorrect evaluation. When a correct answer is given, the guided practice tool should (1) confirm the correctness of the answer, and (2) offer a brief statement of the rationale for the answer.

  This feedback should center on the logic or reasoning that leads to the correct response. Such a reference will reinforce the learner's correct thinking or will correct the wrong thinking of a student who selects the correct answer by incorrect reasoning or a lucky guess.

Remember these guidelines for good feedback to incorrect answers:

1. Never chide the learner. Negative feedback — especially language that questions the learner's abilities — serves only to discourage the learner and often leads to an "early exit" from the drill exercise. Focus on the logic leading to the response rather than any personal qualities of the responder.

2. Identify faulty reasoning. Questions should be carefully constructed to anticipate the most common errors in learner reasoning. Feedback should point out these logical mistakes in incorrect responses and then draw the learner to correct logic for answering the question. Feedback on wrong responses must explain why the answer was wrong.

3. Anticipate technically correct but wrong answers. Students who are equipped with all the skills and information to answer a question may nevertheless offer an incorrect response through a typing error, misspelling, or alternative form of the correct answer. Well-crafted questions offer complex answer judging — the recognition of a variety of acceptable responses, including the most common misspellings of an answer. In such cases, the feedback should evaluate the content of the answer as correct, but identify the technical error and supply the correct form of the answer.

- Sensitivity to Learning Level

  Exercises need to show sensitivity to repeated learner success or failure and adapt question levels to learner needs. If a learner has succeeded in answering 10 successive questions demonstrating a specific skill, it is time-consuming and frustrating to force the learner to complete 100 questions. The same is true if a learner has failed to answer the same ten questions successfully.

  Guided practice exercises also show sensitivity to learner success or failure by providing early exit options and qualitative leaps to more difficult or less difficult questions. If all questions in an exercise reflect the same difficulty level, provide an early exit opportunity.

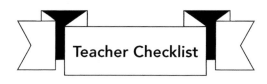

Teacher Checklist

Homework

Yes   No

☐   ☐   Expectations for homework are clearly explained in advance.

☐   ☐   Parents are informed about expectations for homework and their support solicited for encouraging completion of homework.

☐   ☐   Homework relates directly to other work in the classroom.

☐   ☐   Homework assignments relate to student interests and background.

☐   ☐   Consistent levels of homework are maintained.

☐   ☐   Students are given timely feedback on the quality of their work.

☐   ☐   Homework assignments challenge students to think in addition to completing repetitive tasks.

☐   ☐   Portions of homework challenge talented students to go beyond and learn more challenging material.

☐   ☐   Assistance is provided for students who are having difficulty completing homework.

☐   ☐   Parents are informed of the quality of homework completed.

Worksheets

Yes   No

☐   ☐   A variety of types of questions are used. Worksheets are easy to read and directions are clear.

☐   ☐   Worksheets include only as much repetition as necessary.

☐   ☐   Additional, more challenging tasks are available to students.

☐   ☐   Worksheets encourage the use of such resources as libraries, reference materials, and encyclopedias.

☐   ☐   Worksheets have a specific purpose tied to the overall instructional plan.

☐   ☐   Worksheets are neat and attractive.

Computer- or Mobile Device-Based Drill and Practice

☐   ☐   The educational objectives are clear.

☐   ☐   Students are challenged appropriately.

☐   ☐   Graphics and sounds don't distract from learning.

☐   ☐   Students are given feedback as to their progress (both positive and negative).

☐   ☐   The software allows students to exit and return to the same spot.

☐   ☐   The software uses a variety of question types to add interest.

☐   ☐   The software allows students to exit the exercise before the exercise is completed.

APPLICATION

Inquiry

Elements of Inquiry

Inquiry has similarities to other instructional strategies. For example, the instruction should be well planned and should relate to the appropriate learning standards. You should serve as a facilitator of learning rather than a distributor of knowledge and should try to use questions effectively in order to allow students to think more deeply about the problem at hand. By focusing on the three elements of inquiry — intriguing investigations, student discourse, and thoughtful reflection — you can better construct inquiry learning in your classroom.

Intriguing Investigations

Successful initial activities have two requirements. They must be interesting enough to capture student attention, and they must pose problems that generate additional questions. You can find many types of situations that make intriguing investigations. Problems, current events, students, the school itself, the community, and "what if" scenarios can be used to create intriguing investigations. In mathematics, you might use a complex math problem. In science, you may select a natural phenomenon and have students explore why it happens. In history it could be a "what if" scenario that changes the course of history which stimulates student questions. And in English, younger students might predict the end of a story while older students might modify a work of literature based on a different author's style.

Student Discourse

The second element in inquiry learning is student discourse. This requires that students be able to work in groups. Successful groups create positive opportunities for students to get feedback and encouragement from their peers for their tentative questions, observations, and solutions. By using group discussions, you can provide multiple learning opportunities for students and, at the same time, create an environment in which not all feedback has to involve you. However, it is vitally important that students have first developed the competence to work effectively in a group. If a class has not had experience in working in cooperative discussion groups, you must devote time to defining the roles and guidelines of group work and to helping students understand and practice participating in discussion groups.

It is in the process of active discourse that inquiry occurs. While each student develops his/her own thoughts and questions, the group context allows these questions to be analyzed and explored as the group seeks detailed observations and solutions through discourse and discussion. It is through such discourse that vague, tangential ideas are either converted into solid, precise understandings or discarded.

Thoughtful Reflection

An intriguing observation followed by rich student discussion is what starts students on a journey of inquiry. The next critical element in constructing an effective inquiry lesson is to create opportunities and express expectations for students to reflect on their own thoughts, ideas, and questions. Group discourse shapes students' ideas, but reflection firmly establishes these new concepts in their minds.

There are several ways you can foster thoughtful reflection. One way is to designate a portion of group discussion time for personal reflection. By expecting students to reflect on their work and by reinforcing good practice, you can motivate students to think about the quality of their observations and questions. You should particularly encourage students to offer recommendations for improving the next inquiry opportunity. Another technique you can use to stimulate reflection is to have students write about their inquiry activities. Journals provide a good forum for students to engage in regular and thoughtful writing. Writing about their experiences allows students to organize their thoughts better and leads to higher quality thinking.

Teacher Behaviors

The three inquiry elements give you observable activities to plan, prepare for, and carry out. These elements are necessary for inquiry, but they are not sufficient. The behaviors listed below are the vital nutrients that bring the elements of inquiry to life. To achieve an effective inquiry environment, cultivate these habits.

1. **Create a culture in which everyone is expected to learn well.**

   - Establish expectations of performance early and make them clear.

   - Display expectations for and models of quality work and procedural guidelines so that they are constant reminders to everyone.

   - Form groups of students with varying abilities.

   - Always expect the best of students. Don't let previous performance or negative reputations influence your actions.

   - Always look for positive aspects in students' work.

   - Reflect on your behaviors continually as you interact with students. Give equal opportunities to all students.

2. **Provide rich and varied resources and learning experiences.**

   - Learning results from stimulation. The more exposure students have to objects, observations, and experiences, the more they will learn.

   - As a facilitator of learning, you need to pay attention to the "stuff" of education. Be vigilant about identifying materials that could be brought into the classroom to stimulate student inquiry.

   - Don't expect textbooks to be the sole source of learning. Look for real-world materials that will engage students.

   - Frame lessons with questions about phenomena, systems, or current events that are interesting and familiar to students.

   - Strive to make connections between disciplines through the use of real-world activities.

   - Be creative in finding ways to make topics interesting to students. Find ways to give students real-world experiences and opportunities for observation. Think about how to bring real-world objects into the classroom for students to work with. Be outrageous, but NEVER compromise the safety of your students. Some creative variations on traditional themes are:

     - Instead of measuring manageable objects, measure the dimensions of the school property or the height of trees on the playground.

     - Instead of creating a tabletop Iroquois longhouse, convert a corridor of the school into a life-size longhouse.

     - Instead of asking students to analyze word problems concerned with fabricated data, have students collect their own data based on hypotheses about their world. For example, who has more pockets in their clothes, boys or girls?

- Ask open-ended questions to open students' minds and stimulate reflection. Some good question phrases are: "Why do you think . . . ?" "What evidence do you have . . . ?" and "How would you explain . . . ?"

- Ask imaginative questions that compel students to look at current information in different ways and from different perspectives.

3. **Focus on individual students' learning progress and specific performances.**

   - Learning is a very personal experience, and students require personal feedback if they are to experience growth in learning. Your fundamental challenge is to make each student in a large, diverse classroom feel like an important individual.

   - Elicit responses that uncover what students know or think about a topic by encouraging them to think about previous experiences or other observations.

   - Find opportunities to observe individual students efforts and recognize achievements.

   - Make a mental note of the achievement of individual students and compliment them at the appropriate time.

4. **Respond appropriately to student questions, accounts, and other work.**

   - Use focused questions, rather than hints or suggestions, to redirect students' investigations when necessary.

   - Before responding to a student's question, be sure that the rest of the class has heard and understood the question.

   - Consider the following options in responding to a question:
     - Expect and encourage students to use their own reasoning to seek solutions and explain their answers. This will allow students to rely less upon you as the sole authority for answers.

- Redirect the question to the class. This strategy helps to promote student-to-student interaction and lessens students' dependence on you as the exclusive source of information.

- Assist the student to answer his/her own question. This may require some prompting to help the student remember previously learned information, or it may require asking the student a more basic question to begin the thought process. This strategy can help students learn how to search for answers on their own, but it is important to be sensitive to the possibility of embarrassment or intimidation, which may discourage students from asking questions in the future.

- Answer the question yourself. This strategy is best when you have little time remaining in class. The disadvantage of this approach is that you do not encourage student-to-student interaction or deeper inquiry and reflection.

- Ask the student to stop after class to discuss the question. This strategy is most appropriate when a student raises a complicated, tangential question or when a student is obviously the only one who does not understand something and a simple answer does not clarify the point. You should be careful, however, to ensure that other students are not having the same problem before moving on to a new topic or question.

- Never fake an answer. If you do not know the answer to a student's question, admit that you can't answer the question and then select one of these or another strategy that you find appropriate:

  - Suggest a resource where the student can find the information. The resource may be written material, another staff member or student, or someone from the community.

  - Volunteer to find the answer yourself and report back to the class. Make sure you actually do return with the answer if you choose this option.

5. **Use questions to expand and deepen students' thinking.**

   - Use questions that stress deeper understandings of "big" ideas and problem-solving skills.

   - Work with other teachers to create a list of good open-ended questions. Don't just "wing it" with questions that pop into your head at the spur of the moment.

   - When using open-ended questions, give students time to think. Have students first think about the question on their own and then discuss their ideas in groups of two or three. This will enable them to think through their ideas before responding in front of the class.

   - Allow three to five seconds of wait-time following questions. Easy questions require less wait-time, perhaps only three seconds. Higher-level questions may require five seconds or more. With particularly complex questions, some instructors will ask students to spend two or three minutes considering the question and noting ideas.

   - Maintain eye contact when a student is speaking. Use non-verbal gestures to indicate your understanding, confusion, or support. Do not interrupt even if you think the student is heading toward an incorrect conclusion.

   - Call students by name rather than pointing in their general direction. This avoids confusion as to who was called on and also helps create a positive climate in which students feel that you know them as individuals.

   - Use active listening. Wait for a second or two following a student's response, paraphrase long answers, and check with the student to be sure that your perception of the response is accurate.

6. **Use appropriate assessment.**

   - Assessments used to measure student progress must reinforce the elements of inquiry, and emphasize the same level of understanding expected of students during instruction. Interesting inquiry-based instructional activities will quickly evaporate if the test that students take does not require the same level of thought and questioning.

- Do not avoid tests that ask students to demonstrate conceptual understanding. Assessments should reflect a balance that reinforces both the behaviors you expect students to develop and the knowledge you expect them to acquire.

- A portion of students' grades should be based on the quality of their work in making observations, posing questions, and contributing to student discourse. Another portion of the assessment should be based on students' demonstration of conceptual understanding.

- Many types of authentic assessments are best administered at the same time that students are completing an inquiry. Don't wait for a certain time to give a test. Use objective evaluations of the quality of student work made during the actual inquiry as part of the assessment.

Teacher Checklist

Intriguing Investigations

Yes No

☐ ☐   Initial activities were intriguing problems rather than simple demonstrations or student exercises.

☐ ☐   Initial activities were grounded in real-world experiences whenever possible.

☐ ☐   Initial activities were well planned, introduced clearly, and interesting to students.

☐ ☐   Initial activities left unanswered questions, prompting students' own questioning.

Student Discourse

☐ ☐   Students were actively engaged.

☐ ☐   Students asked good questions.

☐ ☐   Students talked to each other — disagreeing, challenging, and debating.

☐ ☐   Students were willing to take risks to push the limits of their learning.

☐ ☐   Students listened to each other and respected one another's opinions.

☐ ☐   Students explained their ideas clearly and precisely.

☐ ☐   Students exhibited confidence in their observations, opinions, and ideas.

Thoughtful Reflection

Yes	No	
☐	☐	Students were able to reflect on their experience and identify what was hard or easy for them, what worked and what didn't, and what they liked and didn't like.
☐	☐	Students used various communication tools to express their ideas.
☐	☐	Students took time to think about the problem, question, or idea that was posed.
☐	☐	Students were able to reflect clearly on the inquiry in a written format.

Teacher Behaviors

☐	☐	Students' desks and the classroom as a whole were arranged to facilitate discussion.
☐	☐	Students were encouraged to show respect for and listen to other students.
☐	☐	Interaction with students encouraged them to take risks, ask questions, and take pride in their work.
☐	☐	Responses to students' questions nurtured the generation of additional questions.
☐	☐	The classroom had a spirit of engaging spontaneity.
☐	☐	I asked thought-provoking, open-ended questions.
☐	☐	I posed genuine questions for which I did not know the answers.
☐	☐	I asked testing questions to find out what my students know.

Yes   No

☐   ☐   I asked focusing questions that encouraged students to think further about an idea — to explain, justify, or hypothesize.

☐   ☐   I used wait-time before and after I received responses to questions.

☐   ☐   I explored ways to pursue student inquiry in relation to each instructional situation.

☐   ☐   I modeled inquiry.

☐   ☐   The classroom atmosphere encouraged students to ask questions.

☐   ☐   Inquiry assessments reinforced students' communication skills by giving them feedback on their writing and speaking.

☐   ☐   Students were assessed at appropriate times during the inquiry.

☐   ☐   Assessment criteria were known to students in advance.

☐   ☐   Assessment included feedback to students on areas that need improvement.

KNOWLEDGE

APPLICATION

Instructional Technology — Independent Learning

Selecting Interactive Software Applications

There are many examples of technology that are used to enhance instruction. This category of instructional technology is where computer software creates a self-contained independent learning environment for the student. These are usually in the form of well-constructed learning systems that function independently of any teacher. The student interacts exclusively with the content of the application and engages in a learning environment to explore new information, acquire new information, analyze problems, and create solutions. In order to be highly engaged, these environments usually incorporate extensive amounts of multimedia and branching, hierarchical learning as the student continues to become proficient. Many of these applications emulate computer games.

Learning independently with technology is usually supplementary instructional programs in schools, which might provide additional work for gifted or more advanced students.

Software is a rapidly changing commodity, with new products appearing daily. As computers and mobile devices become more powerful, they are able to handle more complex software. You may need to devote considerable time to searching out, reviewing, and evaluating software to find applications that create the desired type of learning. Not all software applications are created equal. Quality educational software that creates opportunities for students to explore and discover independently has the characteristics listed below.

Student Control. Students should be in control of the learning process through the software application. Software applications may recommend what path to take, but students should always be able to stray from it to pursue their own interests and curiosity. The software should allow students to dig deeper into ideas, concepts, and applications. The metaphor of "peeling the onion" is appropriate. As the student uncovers one level of information, a new level appears which can be explored as well.

Provide a Safe Place to Fail. In some situations, it is unrealistic or dangerous to allow novices to practice in real situations. Computers and mobile devices can offer realistic simulations that provide a safe environment in which to make and learn from mistakes without embarrassment. This aspect of trial and error is a natural part of normal learning. The software should allow students to experiment and learn from failures.

Start with Problems, then Explanations. Students respond best when they see how what they are told relates to problems with which they are struggling. Applications should create problems for students to examine and then at the proper time offer explanation. Instruction must clearly and directly address the real needs of students to solve the problem at hand.

Make the Subject the Focus. Several popular math software applications adopt a game mentality where mathematics is not the center of the focus. The game involves solving a mystery or accumulating points, and math problems are provided as barriers to be overcome in completing the game. This type of software lacks the advertised mathematical concepts of understanding numbers and computation as its focus. Mathematics is really a peripheral part of the software. Truly interactive software has the education purpose as its central focus. In the case of mathematics, students must be challenged to think and explore math concepts.

Navigation to Answers. Software that instructs but does not let students ask questions removes control from students' hands. Students should be able to ask questions of the educational software they are using and expect reasonable replies. Often, however, students do not know what question to ask. In this case, it should be possible for students to navigate through an information base so as to discover what is there.

Evaluating Software. You need to be able to evaluate whether a software application will meet your curriculum objectives as well as how the software will impact student learning. The results from integrating technology instruction in classrooms and learning labs will only be as good as the software chosen for students.

Software evaluation can be broken up into smaller, easily analyzed components. The components are: (1) educational value, (2) learner engagement, and (3) independent learning. When you critique these components, you will be able to judge the educational value of the software. The best way to evaluate any software is to critique each component separately. This will allow you to concentrate on one area of the program without interference from the other components.

1. Educational Value

Simply having engaging applications does not mean students will grasp the objectives of the curriculum. You must evaluate the software's value to the students and its educational soundness. Is the software consistent with sound teaching principles, learning, and cognition? Are the objectives expressed in terms of the learner's behavior? To provide educational value software must be able to perform in a capacity that meets the curriculum objectives.

Graphics and sound should not detract from the program's educational intentions, and feedback should be relevant, with meaningful graphics and sound capabilities. The program should grow with the student and offer a broad challenge range as well as provide strategies to extend the learning. You need to ask, "What can the student learn from this program?" and "Is the learning meaningful and in line with what I have set up as a goal to meet my curriculum objectives?"

All educational software and applications should be designed to implement some form of evaluation for you. Allowing you to record a student's history of program use over a period of time meets this need. You can then evaluate how a student is using the program, what progress has been made, and at what level the student is performing. It also provides documentation of areas where the student may need additional help or instruction. The software should also include speech features, printing features, and adjustable sound levels. Feedback should be customized and presented in some way to the student. It is also beneficial to have software that is complemented by student workbooks or printable activities for use during or after the computer experience.

Ask yourself this question: Does the software allow the student to begin at any point in the program, or does the student always need to start at the beginning? It is helpful if the student can start where he/she left off last time. Good software has features that allow students to start at many points. This is important because each student may have only minimal time to use the computer.

2. Learner Engagement

If we want students to use the application, it must be not only educational but also entertaining. A level of fun involved in the educational experience will motivate students to use the software repeatedly. Entertaining educational software should include graphics, speech, and sounds that are meaningful to students and appeal to a wide audience. The program should provide a fluid challenge that allows students to select from a range of difficulty levels. To be entertaining and educational, the software must also be responsive to the students' actions.

The ideal software package is one that can be easily used by students with minimal help or instruction. Students should be able to manipulate the software independently after the initial introduction. Look at the software to determine that the skills needed to operate it are in the developmental range of your students.

To be easy to use, the software application must:

- be easy to navigate and have straightforward menus
- use large icons that are easy to select
- let students move in and out of activities quickly at any time

3. Independent Learning

While interactive applications should engage students with attractive graphics, the ultimate test is whether the software application allows the student to move independently through many layers of exploration. These multiple levels create the rich learning environment that supports the individual learning styles and interests of students. If the interactive system is going to be a significant part of the students learning, it needs to foster independent exploration.

Conclusion

The ideal software package will integrate all of the above-mentioned criteria. Of course, it is very unlikely that you will find many software packages or applications that include every desired feature. You need to be able to make educated judgments when reviewing software for classroom implementation. If you judge software based on its educational soundness and not its wow factor, you can integrate technology as a useful and beneficial part of the educational process.

Context of Technology-based Learning

- Learning through multimedia software should not completely isolate students from interaction with other students. Look for instructional activities that include student interaction in addition to being effective software.

- Virtual reality situations provide learners with models of ways to solve real-world problems. On the other hand, learning that is too tightly coupled to a virtual world is fragile. Learning theory reminds us of the importance of interactive communications such as conversation and collaborative problem solving, not just viewing or replicating canned multimedia elements. Look for multimedia applications that have not only sophisticated graphics but also features promoting collaboration.

- Effective technology-based instruction "scaffolds" learning by structuring the user's contributions and decisions to guide students' browsing gradually to more complex tasks. If software does not incorporate scaffolds, you should structure related activities to extend learning opportunities. For example, if a software program has the ability to capture a session history as students work, the session can later be replayed for reflection to encourage higher-order learning in which students become aware of their own process of constructing knowledge.

Teacher Checklist

Selecting Software Applications

Educational Value

Yes   No

☐   ☐   The software meets educational and curriculum objectives.

☐   ☐   The activity is based on problem solving rather than drill.

☐   ☐   Content takes center stage and is not treated as an obstacle to be overcome in order to win the game or get back to the action.

☐   ☐   Children with different learning styles can enter into the activities.

☐   ☐   Activities are built around a coherent and focused set of ideas, leading to progressively deeper thinking.

☐   ☐   The software encourages thoughtful discussion about the content.

☐   ☐   The content is free of gender, ethnic, and religious biases.

☐   ☐   The software responds to the student's own rate of learning.

☐   ☐   The graphics do not detract from the program's educational intentions.

☐   ☐   The software tracks student work to show what the student has learned and progress made.

☐   ☐   You understand how to use the program effectively.

☐   ☐   The program has the capacity to print all relevant items.

Yes   No

☐   ☐   The design contains uncluttered, realistic graphics.

☐   ☐   Your evaluation options are easy to find and use.

Engagement

☐   ☐   The program or application is enjoyable for the student to use.

☐   ☐   All children see their interests reflected in the activities.

☐   ☐   Graphics and sounds are meaningful and enjoyed by students.

☐   ☐   The activities engage students deeply and encourage them to come back again.

☐   ☐   The program or application is appealing to a wide audience.

☐   ☐   The theme of the program is enjoyable and meaningful to students.

☐   ☐   The software is responsive to the student's actions.

Independent Learning

☐   ☐   Students can use the program or application independently after the first use.

☐   ☐   The skills to operate the program are in the developmental range of the students.

☐   ☐   The software provides good navigation; menus and icons are intuitive.

☐   ☐   It is easy for the student to get in and out of activities at any point.

☐   ☐   The program provides extensive branching for students to pursue more advanced content.

☐   ☐   On-screen help and instructions are given.

APPLICATION

Lecture

When to Use a Lecture

Lecture is by far the most popular instructional strategy used by teachers. It is also one of the least engaging strategies for students. When planning a lesson, ask yourself if a lecture is the most appropriate strategy. It can be, if:

- You, the teacher, are the primary source of knowledge on a topic.

- There is considerable and critical knowledge students must know before they begin to work on a problem or activity. For example, a lecture on safety procedures is the best way for students to gain the awareness they need before beginning science lab work.

- Time is limited. Lectures are not always engaging but they are efficient ways to use instructional time.

- You need to change the pace. Effective teaching requires frequently "shifting gears"— changing the activities in which students are engaged. Students struggling through a difficult design or research problem will find a well timed, interesting lecture a welcome change of pace.

- When you have a particularly interesting and appropriate story to share with students, the lecture serves as an effective medium for telling the tale.

- An outside expert or resource person is visiting the class. A lecture may be the most efficient technique for sharing the person's expertise.

Suggestions for Preparing a Lecture

Good lectures don't just happen. They must be planned. Here are some things to do prior to a lecture:

- Know your subject. Study the material thoroughly and only talk about topics you understand well. Lectures that only reiterate textbook passages are ineffective and a waste of everyone's time.

- Prepare several visuals to reinforce the few ideas you want students to remember. Don't make students guess at what is important.

- Develop one or more stories to illustrate the points you are making in the lecture. Stories are an excellent way to reinforce your ideas, since people enjoy listening to and tend to remember stories. These anecdotes need not be humorous. They should not appear to be about you personally.

- Relate the content to the students' previous knowledge or experience. As with all learning, students remember lecture material by making connections to previous experiences.

- Plan your opening carefully. This is when you capture or lose attention. A dramatic demonstration, colorful story, probing question, or powerful visual can spark interest and start your lecture off on a positive note.

Pre-Lecture Activities for Students

The following strategies will help increase student interest prior to a lecture.

- **Reading.** Assign a short piece to read that relates to the lecture topic. Avoid a textbook assignment. Find something in a trade book, in a magazine article, or on the Internet.

- **Case Problem.** Give students a problem related to the topic. Ask them to generate solutions or propose an answer. For example, a case study preceding a lecture on U.S. participation in World War II could ask students to decide whether the United States should enter the World War in Europe in 1941.

- **Opinion Question.** Before you start a lecture, you might pose a question to students, poll their responses, and post them on a visual. For example, before lecturing about a scientific principle, you might ask students their beliefs on a science related myth, such as heavier objects falling faster.

- **Personal Response.** Prior to starting a lecture, give the students a question that relates to the topic and have them write a personal response. For example, prior to a lecture on nutrition, you might ask students to describe the foods someone trying to lose weight might avoid.

- **Puzzle Exercise.** As a warm-up, have students do a puzzle or game that relates to the lecture. For example, you might have students do a word search using key terms from the lecture.

- **Questions.** Have students generate questions in advance. This is particularly useful for a guest lecture. Agree on several questions and have students be prepared to ask them.

- **Structured Note-taking.** Have students use a three-column technique for recording notes on a lecture.

   Facts I Already Know   New Information   Questions I Have

Suggestions During Lectures

These ideas will improve the quality of lectures.

- State the objectives up front. Make it clear why this information is important and how it connects to other learning experiences that preceded or will follow the lecture.

- Be enthusiastic and animated. You cannot expect your students to get excited about a topic for which you appear to have little enthusiasm.

- If you're nervous, write out the first two or three minutes of the lecture. That will carry you until you loosen up.

- Keep it short. Consider the attention span of students. Don't fill a time slot; only spend as much time as necessary. While college lectures are 50–60 minutes, younger students are less likely to stay engaged in a lecture of that length. Keep lectures for elementary students to 10–15 minutes and high school students to 20–30 minutes.

- Avoid standing behind a desk or podium. Move around the room. Stand as close to the audience as possible and still be seen clearly by everyone.

- Make eye contact with each member of the audience at some point.

- Don't read your material. Use a system of brief notes to keep your lecture organized and remind you of key information.

- Avoid personal stories or references. Stories are effective but telling personal stories about yourself is not. "I did this" or "I remember when I was your age" are killers to student interest. Instead, convert those interesting personal experiences to third person stories.

- Limit use of statistics unless students have visuals or handouts to which they can refer. Also, present statistics in graphical form rather that in lists or tables of numbers.

- Watch student body language and other indirect responses. Are students attentive, distracted, or bored? Are they taking notes? Asking questions?

- Be ready to change the pace or do something dramatic to get students' attention. If you see students gazing out the window or heads nodding, find a technique to refocus attention. A visual, question, or sound bite related to the topic is useful, but you could also develop some routine technique for dramatically refocusing the attention of the audience. One teacher periodically tosses a soft rubber Koosh® ball to a student and asks the student to summarize the last point of the lecture.

Use of Visuals

Visuals can increase interest and retention of information in lectures if they are used effectively. There are excellent tools for preparing visuals to enhance lectures. Here are some tips.

- Always prepare visuals in advance. Avoid drawing or writing in front of class. Routinely writing information on a chalkboard or even an overhead projector wastes time and frequently results in visuals that are hard to understand and words that are difficult to decipher.

- Maintain eye contact with the audience by using such visuals devices as overhead, slide, and computer projectors with remote control to reduce interruptions. When you must manipulate the visual, you lose eye contact with the students.

- Be sure your visuals can be seen and read. A frequent error is using visuals that are too small. Letters on visuals must be larger than those normally used for printed material. As a rule, always make sure the font size on overhead transparencies is at least 18 point. Use at least 24 point for computer displays. One way to determine if a transparency can be viewed easily is to place a white sheet of paper behind it and lay in on the floor. If you can read it easily from a standing position, your audience can probably read it.

- Keep visuals simple. Visuals work better if they are limited to a few words or short sentences. Use bullets and key words to convey ideas; avoid paragraphs. Don't put everything you're going to say on your visuals and then read them. Your students can do that for themselves.

- Build your visuals one idea at a time. When showing complex charts or diagrams, use a sequential display of several slides that each adds more detail. Computer displays make this easy to do and contribute to making complex visuals easy to understand.

Questions and Answers

Good lectures stimulate a lively exchange of information through student questions and responses from the lecturer. Poor lectures are void of questions and merely fill the allotted time with teacher talk. The following techniques will help to stimulate student questioning and make lectures more interesting.

- Allot time for questions. Prepare in advance to fill time with additional material if questions don't materialize, but don't eliminate time for questions.

- Wait. Silence may seem like wasted time, but it gives students time to think and generate a question. Don't stop abruptly, ask for questions, and quickly move on if there is no immediate response.

- Encourage questions during a lecture. Don't hold questions until the end.

- Distribute paper and require students to write down a question.

- Compliment the questioner. Refer to the questioner by name and tell him/her that the question is a good one (if it was indeed good).

- Have students form groups to generate a question to ask.

- Give rewards. Include questioning and class participation in grading procedures.

- Listen carefully to questions. The level and focus of questions are clues to the depth of students' understanding. If a student seems embarrassed about asking a basic question, you can say, "I'm glad you brought that up. Probably a lot of people are confused about it."

- Encourage your students to question beyond the information in your lecture. Admit when you don't know something. Instead of bluffing, you can work on the question with the students or bring the answer to the next class.

Suggestions for Improving Lecture Quality

Any lecture can be improved. You should develop a habit of regularly reflecting on the effectiveness of your lectures.

- Periodically record presentations on audiotape or video tape to judge your use of language, speed, and voice.

- Use the "minute paper" (or other assessment techniques). Ask students to respond in one or two sentences to the following questions:

  1. What stood out as most important in today's lecture?

  2. What are you confused about?

Do this for every lecture. It will take you 15 minutes to review the sheets, and you'll learn an enormous amount.

Flipping Your Classroom

A recent trend using technology to improve student engagement is termed "flipping" your classroom. This refers to the fact that traditional instruction is often introduced to students in the form of a lecture followed by some student activity in which they practice or discuss what they've learned in a lecture and then may do additional practice in the form of homework. The lecture becomes a large component of the class instruction and homework becomes practice. In a "flipped" classroom the teacher uses homework as time for students to acquire new information from a lecture. By removing the lecture from the classroom, more time can be devoted in class to student discussion, interaction, and individual support and assistance from students as they reinforce their learning. Teachers provide the lectures in the form of pre-recorded audio or video that are made available to students in the form of podcasts. The homework assignment for students is to view the lecture and then engage in classroom discussion based upon that knowledge.

There is initially additional work for teachers to record lectures. However, over time it proves to be a more efficient use of teacher time, as the lessons are recorded and teachers can devote time to work with small groups of students and check for understanding. The use of flipped classrooms is more personalized and more engaging to students.

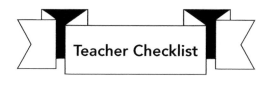

Teacher Checklist

Yes   No

☐   ☐   The lecture was fully prepared and connected to course/grade objectives.

☐   ☐   Lecture was the most efficient strategy to develop these objectives.

☐   ☐   A pre-lecture activity helped to get students engaged in the topic.

☐   ☐   Effective visuals were used for the main points.

☐   ☐   The main points were limited to three to five items.

☐   ☐   Stories were used to illustrate the main points.

☐   ☐   Students were engaged and asked questions.

☐   ☐   A summary at the end highlighted the key purposes of the lecture.

☐   ☐   Information was linked to students' prior knowledge (i.e., common experiences or previous coursework).

☐   ☐   I exhibited enthusiasm for the topic and information.

☐   ☐   Students were given time to think and genuine opportunities to respond.

☐   ☐   I had students assess the lecture.

APPLICATION

Memorization

Memorization as an Instructional Strategy

Memorization is a legitimate and important part of a student's education. The traditional route to memorizing is through rote repetition until the information is firmly planted in memory. Memorizing through repetition takes up so much time, however, that it distracts from the real purpose of learning, which is to understand information.

No one knows precisely what knowledge students will need to know to succeed in the future. Ultimately, it is better to help students develop habits of thinking that will enable them to learn on their own whatever they need to know. Part of becoming a lifelong learner is learning how to memorize information effectively.

The ancient Greeks developed basic memory systems called "mnemonics," a name derived from their goddess of memory, Mnemosene. In the ancient world, a trained memory was an immense asset, particularly in public life, because there were no convenient devices for taking notes.

The Greeks discovered that human memory works by linking things together. Any thought, action, word, or statement can trigger an associated memory.

There are three main components to be considered in memorization:

- Using multiple senses.
- Making an association interesting or familiar.
- Associating items to something already known.

Multiple sensory instruction and interesting, relevant instruction will aid in memory. In addition, the use of memorization techniques or mnemonics will create associations that will enable students to recall critical and important information.

Examples of Mnemonic Devices

The following are several different forms of associations that can be used to memorize information.

Acronym. Form a word or phrase from the first letters of the names you wish to memorize. One example is the word HOMES, an acronym for the five Great Lakes: Huron, Ontario, Michigan, Erie, Superior.

Acrostic. An acrostic is another common mnemonic. It is a phrase or a sentence in which each word begins with the first letter of the items being learned. For example, "Every Good Boy Does Fine" is a mnemonic for the five notes on the treble clef—EGBDF.

Rhyming. Use a rhyming word or simple poem to remember information. For example a common mnemonic to memorize the number of days in a month is "Thirty days hath September, April, June, and November . . . "

Image Links. By making a connection between a word, number, or concept with a vivid image you can easily bridge the gap between the concrete state and the symbolic. You can use a combination of image links and alliterations to remember peoples' names. When you meet someone, focus on a physical feature or manner that starts with same letter as their name. For example, Rhonda — red hair, Justin — jaw, Allison — affable. When you notice the feature again you will recall the name.

A good example of image links comes from the Mind Tools website. If you want to remember a list of counties in the South of England (Avon, Dorset, Somerset, Cornwall, Wiltshire, Devon, Gloucestershire, Hampshire, Surrey) you might develop a series of picture links such as the following (Source: Mind Tools, Inc. www.mindtools.com/March 1999):

- An AVON (Avon) lady knocking on a heavy oak DOOR (Dorset). The DOOR opens to show a beautiful SUMMER landscape with a SETting sun (Somerset).

- The setting sun shines down onto a field of CORN (Cornwall). The CORN is so dry it is beginning to WILT (Wiltshire).

- The WILTing stalks slowly fall onto the tail of the sleeping DEVil (Devon).

- On the DEVil's horn a woman has impaled a GLOSsy (Gloucestershire) HAM (Hampshire) when she hit him over the head with it.

- Now the DEVil feels SORRY (Surrey) he bothered her.

A picture link need not have a sequence of images. All that is important are the images and the links between images.

Story Method. An expansion of the picture link method is to sequence the picture images into a story.

An example of the picture links to remember English counties might go like this (Source: Mind Tools Inc. www.mindtools.com/March 1999):

An AVON lady is walking up a path towards a strange house. She is hot and sweating slightly in the heat of high SUMMER (Somerset). Beside the path someone has planted giant CORN in a WALL (Cornwall), but it's beginning to WILT (Wiltshire) in the heat. She knocks on the DOOR (Dorset), which is opened by the DEVil (Devon). In the background she can see a kitchen in which a servant is smearing honey on a HAM (Hampshire), making it GLOssy (Gloucestershire) and gleam in bright sunlight streaming in through a window. Panicked by seeing the DEVil, the AVON lady panics, screams SORRY (Surrey), and dashes back down the path.

Given the fluid structure of this mnemonic, it is important that the images stored are as vivid as possible and that the significant coding images are much stronger than the ones that merely support the flow of the story.

Number/Rhyme Technique. This technique works by creating mental pictures in which the numbers are represented by things that rhyme with the number and are linked to images that represent the things to be remembered. This is useful when you need to remember items in numerical order or linked to a number.

A typical rhyming scheme for numbers 1–10 is: 1 — Bun, 2 — Shoe, 3 — Tree, 4 — Door, 5 — Hive, 6 — Bricks, 7 — Heaven, 8 — Skate, 9 — Line, 10 — Hen.

If you find that these images do not attract you or stick in your mind, then change them to something more meaningful to you. These images should be linked to images representing the things to be remembered, for example, a list of ten Greek philosophers could be remembered as (Source: Mind Tools, Inc. www.mindtools.com/March 1999):

1. Parmenides — a BUN topped with melting yellow PARMEsan cheese.

2. Heraclitus — a SHOE worn by HERACLes (Greek Hercules) glowing with a bright LIghT.

3. Empedocles — a TREE from which the M-shaped McDonalds arches hang hooking up a bicycle PEDal.

4. Democritus — think of going through a DOOR to vote in a DEMOCRaTic election.

5. Protagoras — a bee HIVE being positively punched through (GORed?) by an atomic PROTon.

6. Socrates — BRICKS falling onto a SOCk (with a foot inside!) from a CRATe.

7. Plato — A PLATe with HEAVEN's angel's wings flapping around a white cloud.

8. Aristotle — a friend called hARRY clutching a bOTtLE of wine possessively slipping on a SKATE.

9. Zeno — a LINE of ZEN Buddhists meditating.

10. Epicurus — a HEN's egg being mixed into an EPileptics's CURe.

Once you have done this, try writing down the names of the philosophers on a piece of paper. You should be able to do this by thinking of the number, then the part of the image associated with the number, then the whole image; finally, you decode the image to give you the name of the philosopher. If the mnemonic has worked, you should be able to recall the names of all the philosophers in the correct order.

Journey System. The journey method is a flexible and effective mnemonic based around the idea of remembering landmarks on a well-known journey. In many ways it combines the narrative flow of the story and the structure and order of the number systems into one highly effective mnemonic.

Because the journey method uses routes that you know well, you can code information to be remembered to a large number of easily visualized landmarks along the routes. Because you know what these landmarks look like, you need not work out visualizations for them!

This route could be your way to school in the morning, the route from one classroom to another, the route to visit a friend, or the way you get to a store. It could even be a journey around the levels of a computer game. Once you are familiar with the technique, you may also be able to create imaginary journeys that fix things in your mind.

Preparing the Route. To use this technique most effectively, it is best to prepare the journey beforehand so that the landmarks are clear in your mind before you try to commit information to them. One way of doing this is to write down all the landmarks that you can recall on your chosen route in order on a piece of paper. This allows you to fix these landmarks as the significant ones to be used in your mnemonic, separating them from others that you may notice on the actual route.

Consider these landmarks as stops on the route. To remember a list of items — people, experiments, events, or objects — associate each thing or representation of a thing with a stop on your journey.

Suppose you want to remember a shopping list: coffee, lettuce, fresh vegetables, bread, paper towels, fish, chicken breasts, pork chops, soup, fruit, bath cleaner, you may choose to associate this with a journey to the supermarket. A series of mnemonic images therefore appears as (Source: Mindtools, Inc. www.mindtools.com/March 1999):

1. Front door: spilt coffee grains on the doormat.
2. A bush in front: growing lettuce and tomatoes around the bush.
3. Car: potatoes, onions, and cauliflower on the driver's seat.
4. End of your street: an arch of French bread over the road.
5. Past garage: sign wrapped in paper towels.
6. Under railway bridge: from which haddock and cod are dangling by their tails.
7. Traffic lights: chickens squawking and flapping on top of lights.
8. Past church: in front of which a pig is doing karate, breaking boards.
9. Under office block: with a soup slick underneath: my car tires send up jets of tomato soup as I drive through it.
10. Past car park: with apples and oranges tumbling from the top level.
11. Supermarket parking lot: a filthy bathtub is parked in the space next to my car!

The system is extremely flexible. To remember many items, use a longer journey with more landmarks. To remember a short list, only use a part of the route.

One advantage of this technique is that you can use it to work both backwards and forwards, and you can start anywhere within the route to retrieve information.

Roman Room. The Roman Room technique is an ancient and effective way of remembering unstructured information where the relationship of one item of information to the other items is not important. It functions by imagining a room you know well. The technique works by associating items with the objects in that room. To recall information, simply take a tour around the room in your mind, visualizing the known objects and their associated images.

For example, imagine a family room or living room as a basis for the technique. In this room, you can visualize the following objects: table, lamp, sofa, large bookcase, small bookcase, CD rack, tape racks, stereo system, telephone, television, chair, mirror, black and white photographs, etc.

To remember this list of World War I war poets, for example, Rupert Brooke, G.K. Chesterton, Walter de la Mare, Robert Graves, Rudyard Kipling, Wilfred Owen, Siegfried Sassoon, and W.B. Yates, walk into the living room and look at the table. On the top is RUPERT the Bear sitting in a small BROOK (we do not need to worry about where the water goes in our imagination!). This codes for Rupert Brooke.

Someone seems to have done some moving. A CHEST has been left on the sofa. Some jeans (Alphabet System: G=Jeans) are hanging out of one drawer, and some cake has been left on the top (K=Cake). This codes for G.K. Chesterton.

The lamp has a small statuette of a brick WALL over which a female horse (MARE) is about to jump. This codes for Walter de la Mare, etc. (Source: Mind Tools, Inc. www.mindtools.com/March 1999)

Memory Techniques

Don't confuse memorizing with comprehending. You might have students memorize dates for a history class or formulas for a math class, but they also need to understand why a date or a formula is significant to the key ideas of the material you are teaching. Before spending vast amounts of time having students memorize details, ask yourself if it would be better to step back and focus on overall comprehension of the big picture.

Here are a few general tips on the use of memory systems to share with students:

- Creative or silly mnemonics often work best because they are easy to remember. Exaggerate size and choose unlikely functions for the image.

- Create your own mnemonics based on your own vivid pictures.

- Use positive, pleasant images. The brain often blocks out unpleasant ones.

- Closing your eyes while trying to visualize an image or story will make it more vivid.

- Be humorous! Funny or peculiar things are easier to remember than normal ones.

- Symbols (red traffic lights, pointing fingers) can be used in mnemonics. The age-old technique of tying a string around your finger really does work.

- Vivid, colorful images are easier to remember than drab ones.

- Use all the senses to code information or dress up an image. Remember that your mnemonic can contain sounds, smells, tastes, touch, movements, and feelings as well as pictures.

- Bringing three dimensions and movement to an image makes it more vivid. Movement can be used either to maintain the flow of association or to help remember actions.

- Remember to use a unique location for each list to separate similar mnemonics. By setting a mnemonic story in one location and clearly using that location as a background, you can separate it from a different mnemonic set in a different place.

- When learning new vocabulary words, use a mnemonic to remember the terms.

You may forget things that you have coded with mnemonics if the images are not vivid enough or if the images you are using do not have enough meaning or strength for you. If this happens, try changing the images to more potent ones.

Retrieving Lost Information

You may find that you need to remember information that either has been lost because part of a mnemonic was not properly coded or simply not placed into a mnemonic. To recall the information, try the following approaches:

In your mind, run through the period when you coded the information, carried out the action, or viewed the thing to be remembered. Reconstructing events like this might trigger associations that will help you to retrieve the information.

If the lost information was part of a list, review the other items on the list. These may be linked in some way to the forgotten item; or even if unlinked, their positions in the list may offer a different cue to retrieve the information.

If you have any information such as general shape or purpose, try to reconstruct the information from this.

If all of the above fail, take your mind off the subject and concentrate on something else completely. Often, the answer will just "pop into your mind," as your subconscious has worked on retrieving the information or something you have been doing sparks an association.

Teacher Checklist

Yes   No

☐   ☐   The information was something that simply must be memorized and did not need to be developed to a deeper understanding.

☐   ☐   When introducing complex new information that needs to be memorized, using a mnemonic technique to remember the information was suggested.

☐   ☐   Students were given a possible mnemonic to help them remember the information.

☐   ☐   Students were given experiences with different types of mnemonic techniques so they could select a system appropriate for the information.

☐   ☐   Students were given practice time with mnemonics to become skillful in using them before needing to remember critical content.

☐   ☐   Students were encouraged to create their own stories and image links that presented vivid images from their own experience.

APPLICATION

Note-taking/
Graphic Organizers

Tips for Helping Students to Take Better Notes

1. Outline Your Lecture

    Be overt in the organization of your lecture, both orally and visually. Use the board to outline important ideas; however, studies show that students usually record what the teacher has written, so be discriminating in your use of the board or transparencies.

    Use signaling phrases and transition statements, such as "this is important," "you'll want to remember," "these differ in three important ways," or "next."

2. Use a Framework

    Give your students a framework or schema for organizing information. Two common frameworks are sequence and classification.

    Sequence may be used to explain change, phases, and stages of growth and can be illustrated easily with arrows connecting one idea with the next in a sequential flow. If the information contains parts, characteristics, elements, etc., you can classify the material and present it in a chart form. Both of these frameworks assist students in comparing, contrasting, and determining similarities and differences in the information.

3. Tell Students What to Record in Their Notes

In the early weeks of class, provide explicit instructions for students on what to record in their notes. The substance of notes may vary from class to class. Students need assistance in determining whether or not to record dates, sample problems, research cited, solutions to problems, questions raised, etc.

4. Guide Students on How to Take Better Notes

Give students feedback. Review their notes occasionally and give suggestions for improvement. If a student comes to you for academic assistance, ask to see his/her class notes. Inadequate notes may be the source of the academic deficiency. Hand out your version of the notes after a class so that students may make a comparison with their own.

5. Provide Time for Note-taking in Class

Use note-taking as a means to encourage students to think about the lecture content. If you show that you value note-taking and provide attention and time to this during your class, students may not only take notes more frequently but also improve their note-taking skills. Many students will learn more by taking and reviewing notes.

Note-taking Strategies

Instruct students on the following tips for improving note-taking skills.

Preparation

- Use a large, loose-leaf notebook. Use only one side of the paper. This way you can take the pages out to "see" the whole thing at once.

- Draw a vertical line about 2–3 inches from the left side of the paper. This is the recall column. Keep all notes to the right of this margin. Use the recall column later to record key words, phrases, questions, and comments about the topic.

- Date and label note pages.

- Know what the topic is before you begin to listen; this helps you to keep focused on the topic.

- Sit where there are few distractions, where you can more easily hear, see, and attend to the material.

During the Lecture

- Outline; indent supporting details and examples under main ideas.

- Capture general ideas; paraphrase and summarize. Don't try to copy sentences verbatim except when definitions and formulas are given.

- Abbreviate (e.g., &, imp., WWII for World War II) and skip unimportant words; asterisk (*) or underline important points. Use symbols: +, =, &, @.

- Write legibly but don't worry about neatness. Use "highlighting" to signify important points.

- Practice the TLQL Technique:
  - *Tune-in* — Listening takes energy.
  - *Look at the Speaker* — Mannerisms will give extra clues to important points, and looking helps you focus your attention.
  - *Question* — Nothing will generate interest so much as an appropriate question.
  - *Listen* — Be alert for speaker emphasis through tone or gesture, repetition, use of cue words such as remember, most important, etc.

- Note especially ideas that are in opposition to your own. These ideas are difficult to understand initially and so require extra effort. People remember things that support their existing concepts and tend to forget those things that disagree with them.

After the Lecture

- Read through your notes and make them more legible if necessary. Rewrite incomplete or skimpy parts in greater detail; fill in gaps that you may recollect.

- Use the column to the left of your notes to record key words or ideas. You will need to reread the teacher's ideas and then reflect them in your own words. When you cover up your notes to show only the recall column, you have a review.

- Relearning is rapid if regular review is used. Review your notes periodically. Compare the information in your notes with your own experience.

- Be critical but also be willing to hold some seeming inconsistencies in your mind over a period of time. Make meaningful associations and memorize what must be memorized.

Using Graphic Organizers in Instruction

Graphic organizers are excellent instructional aids; however, some are more suitable for certain content and types of information than others. Determining which graphic organizer to use and selecting the appropriate information to record on the organizer affect the value of the graphic organizer to the learner.

Graphic organizers have a number of instructional uses. These include:

- locating and remembering key ideas and information
- introducing text information
- summarizing learning units or chapters
- grasping information as a whole
- drawing interrelationships among ideas
- serving as alternative test formats
- providing study guides

As a beginning exercise, make a list of the various types of graphic organizers, analyze the content you teach, and match instructional topics with different forms of the organizers on your list.

Choosing Appropriate Graphic Organizers

Think about the need for and appropriateness of a visual tool as it relates to the ultimate learning goal. Some essential questions to consider when choosing graphic organizers as a part of your instruction include:

1. *Which type will best support the purpose of the lesson?* The learning goal and student expectations are essential considerations when selecting a graphic organizer. For example, if you want students to generate ideas for a writing exercise, a clustering web could be used. If you want students to show the cause and effect of multiple factors and their interrelationship on an event or idea, then a fishbone diagram would be appropriate.

2. *Which graphic organizer is developmentally appropriate?* Once you identify the organizer that correlates with your instructional purpose, then you need to consider the form and procedures that are appropriate for the developmental level of your students. At the elementary level, the graphic needs to be large, and instructions may need to be given verbally as well as in writing. Colored markers and crayons become the tools for completing the forms. At this level, a few visual forms, such as triangles, squares, or circles, are best. Too many forms will distract and confuse the learners and they will lose interest. For middle school and secondary students, steps for using the tools need to be clearly explained so that students may work independently to design and use the graphics. Computer software programs for visual learning and graphic organizers are very appropriate and motivating at this level.

3. *How will the class use this tool?* It is important to know how you intend the class to interact with the graphic organizer. Will students use the organizer individually, in pairs, or in groups? Will it be a part of whole group instruction or will it be included in a facilitated learning activity? Maybe it will be a combination of approaches. The selection needs to account for these options.

4. *How will the effectiveness of this organizer be assessed?* After using a graphic organizer, it is important to reflect on its usefulness and effectiveness in student understanding and learning.

5. *Are graphic organizers going to be used throughout the year as a part of instruction and student learning activities?* If you are going to use graphic organizers and expect students to use them, it is important that you make this clear to students. If you eventually want your students to be able to use graphic organizers independently and as easily as writing, then you need to demonstrate and reinforce them frequently.

Designing Graphic Organizers

Follow these guidelines when designing graphic organizers:

1. Identify the information to be depicted on the organizer.
2. List the main idea and key points to be included.
3. Choose an appropriate organizing format.
4. Show interrelationships among points.
5. Include items that require higher-level thinking skills.
6. Show items that present a summary or synthesis of the whole lesson.
7. Include enough information for the student to reconstruct the original information.
8. Use adequate connecting lines.

Assisting Students to Design Graphic Organizers

The most effective way to have students design and use graphic organizers is to teach with them. Model their use for students. Have students design the organizer with you as a part of instruction. Use the following guidelines:

1. Introduce students to graphic organizers by explaining and showing what they are and how they can be used to depict information.

2. Give students effective and non-effective examples of graphic organizers. Pull the information for these from material that students are familiar with or have just studied.

3. Use graphic organizers or fill them in as you teach.

4. Have students complete the organizer as you teach.

5. Provide students with a template of the graphic organizer you are using in instruction. Complete the organizer with students.

6. Have students work in small groups to complete graphic organizers. Have groups complete more than one organizer for the same information. Discuss the different emphasis portrayed by the organizer chosen.

7. Give students opportunities to create their own graphic organizers.

8. Have students present their organizers to the class and explain the formats they selected.

Types of Graphic Organizers

Describing

Brainstorming Web. A brainstorming web starts with a core concept, or main idea, at its center. Information related to the main idea is identified in a free-flowing manner and radiates outward from general to specific, linking related ideas.

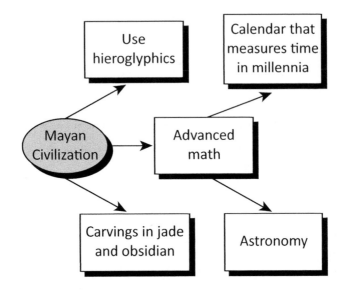

Clustering Web. Clustering generates ideas, images, and feelings around a stimulus word. One idea builds on another, enabling students to enlarge and categorize their ideas for writing and to see patterns in their thoughts. The clustering web differs from the brainstorming web in that ideas are grouped in logical categories or clusters.

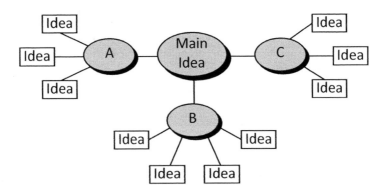

Character Web. A character web represents a character in a work of literature. It depicts the character's traits and can include quotations that illustrate those traits.

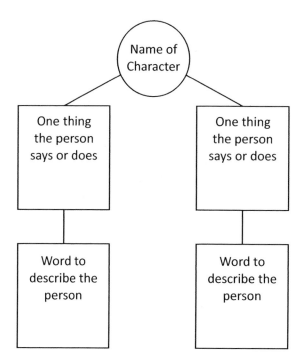

Hierarchy. A hierarchy shows connections between people or objects in a system of ranking one above another. These might represent groupings, such as animal species, or show a traditional organization chart. Another type of hierarchy is a family tree, which shows how family members are related.

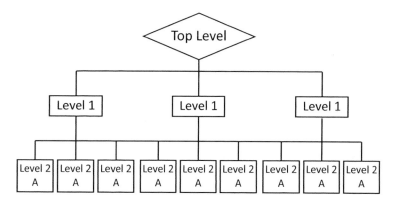

Continuum. A graphic organizer is a simple tool to illustrate a sequence of events. It is used to show timelines of historical events, degrees of something, shades of meaning (Likert scales), or rating scales. The main organizers are what is being scaled and the extremes or end points. This might be used for a listing of major wars or events that occurred in a story.

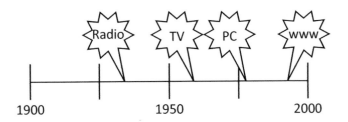

Spider Map. The spider map is used to describe a central idea, process, thing, concept, or proposition. It is useful for brainstorming ideas and to organize thoughts for a writing project. The main ideas are illustrated as well as their attributes or functions.

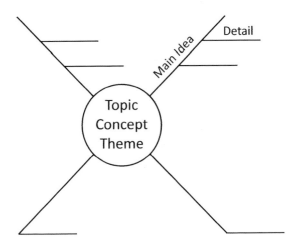

Solving Problems

Affinity Diagram. This graphic sorts many ideas into logical groupings. Solving problems or making decisions frequently starts with generating a long list of ideas. The affinity diagram leads to more thoughtful analysis by sorting and labeling these ideas.

What are the issues involved in successfully marketing our holographic phones?

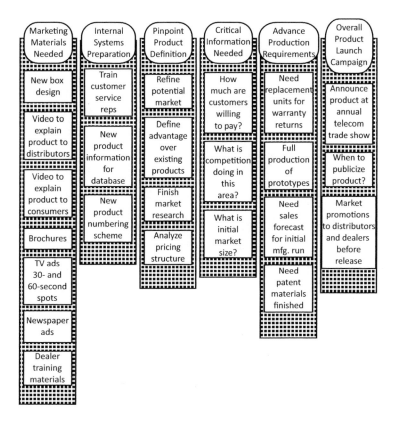

Cause and Effect (Fishbone Map). This graphic organizer, sometimes called a fishbone map, is often used for problem solving. It is helpful in analyzing changes, conflicts, and the causes-and-effects of events or situations. The factors involved in the problem or event and their interrelationship are identified and recorded. The varied causes are analyzed, ordered, and prioritized as to the most rational conclusions.

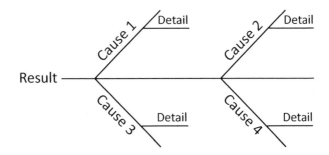

Media Plan. This is a graphic, sequential depiction of a narrative. Students recall major events of the story, then illustrate the events in the squares provided.

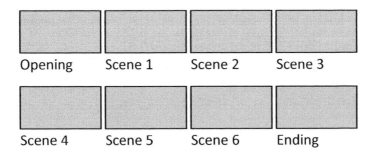

Decision Matrix. This graphic organizer is useful for evaluating possible solutions to a problem. Several criteria are identified to rate the alternative solutions. These are organized in a matrix. Each alternative solution is evaluated against each criterion. This systematic evaluation and graphic presentation of alternative solutions can lead to easier decision making.

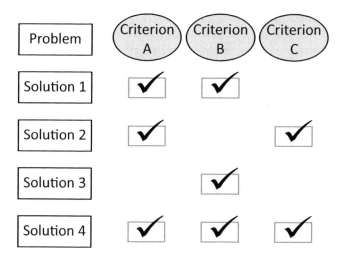

Making Meaning

Concept Map. This is used to show connections among complex ideas (e.g., democracy) or branching procedures (e.g., the circulatory system). Key questions: What is the superordinate category? What are the subordinate categories? How are they related? How many levels are there?

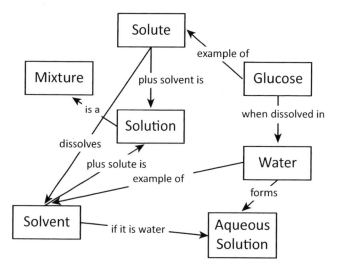

Cycle. The cycle graphic organizer shows how a series of events interact to produce a set of results that repeat. Some examples of this would be weather patterns, the life cycle, cycles of achievement and failures. The cycle depicts the responses to the main events in the cycle.

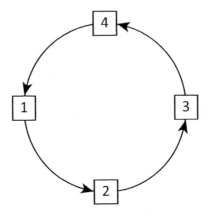

KWL Chart. KWL stands for Know, Want to Know, and Learned. This chart helps students activate prior knowledge, pinpoint knowledge needed, and reflect on learning.

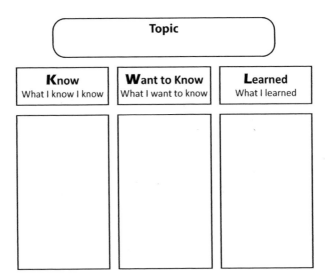

Interaction Outline. An interaction outline is used to show the nature of an interaction between persons or groups, such as the interaction between European settlers and American Indians. The graphic depicts a response to the persons or group. What were their goals? Did they conflict or cooperate? What was the outcome for each person or group?

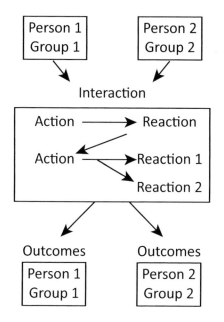

T-Graph. This is used to show similarities and differences between two things (people, places, events, ideas, etc.). The graphic shows what is being compared and how they are similar and different.

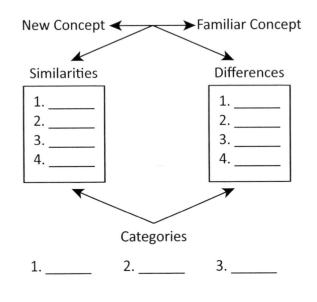

T-Graph

Venn Diagram. This is made up of two or more overlapping circles. It is often used in mathematics to show relationships between sets. In English language arts instruction, Venn diagrams are useful for analyzing similarities and differences in characters, stories, poems, etc. This organizer is an effective pre-writing activity. It helps students to organize thoughts, quotations, similarities and differences visually prior to writing a compare/contrast essay.

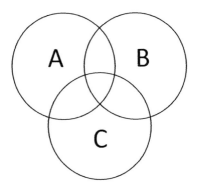

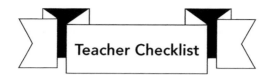

Teacher Checklist

Note-taking

Yes   No

☐   ☐   Students were made aware of the importance of note-taking and its impact on learning.

☐   ☐   You instructed students in effective note-taking procedures.

☐   ☐   You used signaling phrases and transition statements, such as "this is important," to alert students to take notes on the item.

☐   ☐   You used frameworks, diagrams, and graphic organizers to organize your information so that it was easier for students to take notes.

☐   ☐   You provided students with copies of your notes so that they had a model to follow and to compare with their notes.

☐   ☐   Students paraphrased what they wrote in their notes, rewrote definitions, restated relationships, or retold examples in their own words.

☐   ☐   Students explained their notes to other students.

☐   ☐   You gave students feedback on their notes.

☐   ☐   You included time for note-taking activities in class.

Graphic Organizers

Yes   No

☐   ☐   Students understand the various formats and purposes of graphic organizers.

☐   ☐   You used graphic organizers to explain and illustrate relationships found in text material.

☐   ☐   You provided visual links to content learning through graphic organizers.

☐   ☐   You used graphic organizers to assist visual learners to understand abstract concepts.

☐   ☐   Your instructional purpose and your expectations of students determined the type of graphic organizer you included in instruction.

☐   ☐   The developmental level of your students determined the form of your graphic organizer.

☐   ☐   Your choice of the type of graphic organizer was partially based on how the organizer would be used in class.

☐   ☐   You and your students reflected on the usefulness of the graphic organizer.

☐   ☐   You modeled the use of graphic organizers in your instruction.

☐   ☐   Students developed graphic organizers with you and independently.

☐   ☐   You used graphic organizers as alternative test formats.

APPLICATION

Presentations/ Exhibitions

Presentations

Some strategies for successful presentations are discussed below.

- **Analyze the Situation.** Students need to understand the situation that creates the need for the presentation. Who is involved? Where will the presentation be delivered? How does the presentation fit with other learning activities? Thus, the context surrounding the presentation and the audience's perspective may define or limit the content.

- **Analyze the Audience.** Audience response determines the success of an oral presentation. Instruct students to tailor their speeches to their audiences. Effective speakers understand their listeners. What are the backgrounds, knowledge, expectations, and attitudes toward the topic? What kinds of biases might the audience have about the topic or even the presenter? A good presenter knows his/her audience. A receptive relationship develops through the presenter's sincerity and knowledge about the topic. Part of the presenter's success depends on an ability to conform to the audience's expectations with respect to dress, demeanor, choice of language, and attitude toward them and the topic.

- **Define the Objectives.** Instruct students to know exactly what they want to accomplish in the presentation. Having clear outcomes in terms of what the audience is to learn or do as a result of the speech will give it purpose. A good presenter knows at the start where he/she wants to end up. Focus throughout the presentation should be on what is to be accomplished by the presentation. An effective technique is to state the goal in one sentence. At the beginning of the speech to give the audience the purpose up front and a sense of what will follow. Restating the purpose in terms familiar to the audience helps to keep content related to the listener.

- **Create the Opening.** It's true! You only have one chance to make a first impression when giving a presentation. Remind students of the importance of starting on time, establishing credibility, having a poised demeanor, and showing energy and enthusiasm for the topic and the task.

- **Outlining the Content.** Preparing for a presentation is similar to writing a report. Students need to recognize that this may require research. Have students determine what information is needed and what will appeal to the audience? Offering various kinds of information will help sustain the listener's interest. Some types to consider include narratives, illustrations, case studies, statistics, personal experiences, and history or background. Similar to written reports, oral presentations are organized around an introduction, body, and conclusion. The introduction gives a preview of the speech and sets the purpose. The body develops the points outlined in the introduction, and the closing restates the main ideas presented and reinforces the purpose. Designing the closing is especially important since people remember best what they hear last. Effective speakers bring power and purpose to their closing remarks. The conclusion answers such questions as "So what?" or "Now what?"

- **Add Spice.** Humor, cartoons, gimmicks, testimonials, analogies, demonstrations, etc., can add the extra something to engage the audience. Students should be encouraged to use their creativity in designing ways to heighten audience interest and participation.

- **Choose an Appropriate Style.** Remind students that how they sound is just as important as what they say. Discuss tone, image, diction, language, approach, and degree of formality. Good speakers sound confident, sincere, respectful, and courteous. The most effective style is conversational. The speaker wants the members of the audience to feel as if he/she is talking to them.

- **Design Visual Aids.** Visuals aids enhance the presenter's ideas. If used effectively, visual aids can make a presentation more persuasive and interesting. Students should keep in mind that visual aids will help their audience understand and follow their ideas, show relationships among ideas, and help the audience to remember what is being said. A variety of visual aids can be used: drawings, graphs, props and objects, charts, blackboard, demonstrations, pictures, statistics, cartoons, photographs, maps, etc. Encourage students to use anything that will help people think in pictures—to see what they mean. Visuals need to be simple and easy to read. In preparing a presentation, consider where and when visuals will be most effective.

When creating a visual:

- Avoid having too much information on it.
- Use no more than four colors.
- Ensure that words and graphics convey one idea.
- Use a type size that can be easily read from afar.
- Convey only one concept, or point.
- Make sure the point is immediately evident.

Computer programs such as PowerPoint, Hyperstudio, and Excel give students an opportunity to experiment with graphic design. Also, some websites have visuals that can be used for presentations. Have students use technology whenever possible.

- **Rehearse! Rehearse! Rehearse!** Practice makes perfect. With practice, the speaker becomes comfortable with the content and the actual activity of giving a speech. Explain to students that with rehearsal they will begin to see themselves as accomplished. The more one presents in front of others, the easier it tends to become. Give them many opportunities to make presentations in school.

Presentation Tips

Here are some additional tips for students to consider when making a presentation.

- **Be natural.** The ability to express your own personality is the most important skill in making an effective presentation.

- **Avoid distractions.** Nervousness can make you do things that the audience can hear and may find distracting. Examples include clicking a pen, coughing, clearing your throat or repeating word or phrase, such as "you know" or "okay." Videotape your presentations to analyze your delivery for these distractions. Physical behaviors can also be distracting, such as pacing around the room, swaying, and looking at the ceiling. Practice speeches in a small group and have group members watch for these distractions.

- **Stay in contact with the audience.** Eye contact makes the audience feel that you are interested in them. To know how people are reacting — to know what they agree and disagree with, what they understand, and what they are confused about — you must be able to see them. Looking at the audience and making eye contact may seem easy and natural, but it does take a conscious decision to do so and perhaps a little practice.

- **Establish a pace and tone.** To sound natural, you need to find your own pace and tone.

- **Use notes and outlines.** Most presenters have notes. You don't need to hide them, the trick is to use them sparingly.

- **Summarize main ideas.** Once a point has been covered, summarize it and move on quickly. Restate some essential points for reinforcement but be cautious of too much repetition.

- **Avoid offensive language or content.** Certain topics and some words or expressions may offend the audience members. Be conscious of your audience and try not to offend any member of the group.
- **Be yourself!** That is most important.

Exhibitions

Exhibitions are culminating activities that allow students to demonstrate what they have learned. To help students mount successful exhibitions, consider the elements listed below.

1. **The Prompt.** The prompt is the thing you ask students to do. It is important to have a clear understanding of what students should exhibit. Without this, you cannot develop standards and exemplars. With this, you can guide students into exhibitions that demonstrate identified standards and high degrees of proficiency. Exhibitions often require students to write a research report and give an oral presentation. Sometimes they may include portfolios or require students to create a project. Be broadminded about the kinds of prompts you give students.

2. **Expectations.** Expectations are what you envision students will accomplish. If the exhibition is a culminating activity, it is important to have expectations that reflect the collective visions of educators and community members. To achieve this, involve both in the entire process. Establish a means for representatives from both groups to discuss the meaning of academic achievement in your school community.

3. **Standards.** You need to decide what level of performance is acceptable. Also, quality performance needs clarity of definition. Exemplars should be provided to students. Scoring guides need to be developed for raters, which give criteria for evaluating student performances. Students need to know in advance what the scoring guides contain. A clear delineation of standards and expectations is essential.

4. **Public Context.** Make exhibiting student work a part of the culture of the school. Take every opportunity to put the work out in the open. Scoring guides will be better understood if student work is visible to all. Find ways to engage the public in serving on evaluation panels.

5. **Coaching.** To support and advise students, ensure that they have an adult mentor, coach, or advisor to assist them in preparing quality exhibitions. Train these individuals to monitor student progress, from the topic selected through research, writing, and product production and presentation. Be sure that these individuals are familiar with the exhibition requirements and time lines. With a strong coaching model, you can begin to develop a culture of student-assisted learning.

6. **Reflection.** Have a formal process for students to reflect on the results of their exhibition and to make modifications.

Choosing the Exhibition Topic

The first step in the exhibition process is to choose a topic. The topic must be one that lends itself to research, performance, and/or product construction. Have students consider the following questions to help them select a topic that will likely bring them success.

- **Am I really interested in this topic?**

  The exhibition will take time; thus, the student needs to be interested in the area of focus.

- **Is there sufficient material available on this topic?**

  This will help students avoid topics that are too narrow or specific or perhaps even too current to yield sufficient information.

- **Will the topic lend itself to project/product development?**

  The end result of the exhibition is a performance or tangible product that reflects the background study.

- **Do I want to share this topic with an audience?**

  This forces students to think about how and what they will present during the final public exhibition.

- **Is the topic too broad?**

  The exhibition usually requires more than superficial coverage. Thus, it must be narrow enough to be developed.

- **What other subjects may be linked to the topic?**

  The topic typically involves an integrated educational approach.

- **Am I challenged by the topic?**

  Choosing a topic that offers an opportunity to learn something, to grow, and to explore an area of interest will increase the student's motivation and contribute to high quality.

- **Have I asked others to comment/agree on the topic?**

  Students usually work with a coach or mentor on their exhibition topic. Thus, having a teacher, another student, or other staff member concur with a topic selection will result in choosing a topic that the student can find assistance in developing.

Conducting Research and Writing the Paper

Review with students the purpose of the research portion of the exhibition. This is a time for them to investigate and explore in greater depth their topic of interest. Also, doing the research means that the student will gather additional information from a variety of sources, internalize it, and draw a conclusion about the topic under study.

A task analysis outline can be very helpful to students. The following is an example of a task analysis for research given to eighth grade students involved in exhibitions (Source: Campbell Union School District, Campbell, California):

- **Thesis statement and overview of project** — includes the purpose and intent of the research paper.

- **Brainstorm previous knowledge** — lists everything the student already knows about the topic.

- **Steps to conduct the research** — contains a list of all the tasks needed to be done to complete the research. This may include sites to visit, books and articles to read, individuals to interview, Internet sites to explore, etc. A projected completion date for each step is also identified.

- **Development and organization of the paper** — provides evidence that the topic is thoroughly developed, with specific examples to support the thesis, and is highly organized with effective transitions; the introduction and conclusion relate to the core of the paper.
- **List of sources** — includes the name and other pertinent information of any sources used in the development of the paper.

Research Paper Checklist

Develop a checklist of questions for the students to review and use as a self-check to measure the effectiveness, completeness, and accuracy of their research papers. Areas to include on the checklist are content/organization, use of references, mechanics, and completeness.

The Project

The project gives the student an opportunity to apply the research. This enables the student to create, design, produce, perform, or invent. Remind students of a variety of activities that can be used for a project. Students may perform through dance, music, or other art. They may teach something or engage in another leadership activity. Sports-related and career-related activities also constitute possibilities for projects.

The Presentation

The presentation is the culminating component of the exhibition. Remind students that this gives them an opportunity to reflect and self-evaluate all that they have learned and engaged in during the exhibition experience. Here, the student describes what has been achieved through the various activities of the exhibition — research, writing the paper, completing the project, designing a resume, etc. Typically, students have approximately 15 minutes to present, followed by a 15-minute question-and-answer period. The panel of judges, comprised of teachers, parents, community members, and other students, typically has some knowledge of the field in which the student has focused the exhibition.

To assist the panel of judges, have students develop a brief overview of their work to provide the panel with background information prior to the presentation. Also, have students assemble all written work in a portfolio folder. This should include reflection logs, as well as the final research paper, project descriptions, and any supporting materials such as charts, graphs, etc.

Preparing the Presentation

Encourage students to consider the following questions as they prepare their oral presentation:

- What can you teach your audience about the subject?
- What have you learned as a result of completing the exhibition?
- What problems did you encounter and how did you resolve them?
- How does the work you have completed through the exhibition connect with other learning experienced through life and/or school?
- What questions do you still have unanswered?

Suggested Oral Presentation Outline

1. **Introduction.** Name, welcome, and thank you to the panel members; general overview of presentation; mention of how questions will be answered.

   Some sample phrases for students to complete in giving the overview are:
   - The title of my exhibition is . . . .
   - The main questions I attempted to answer are . . .
   - What I will describe to you today is . . .

2. **Body.** The procedures followed, experts consulted, research, materials gathered. Here the student describes what has been learned and how it was learned. Also, obstacles encountered are related. The most significant part of this section is the conclusions that the student has drawn from his/her work.

3. **Summary.** In this summative section, the student clearly states his/her accomplishment(s) and perhaps shares some things that might have been done differently.

Preparing for Questions from the Panel

Have students brainstorm possible questions that they may be asked. Some typical questions for students to consider are:

- What would you want to know if you were on the panel?
- Why did you choose your topic?
- What questions do you think the judges should ask?
- How much time did you spend on this?
- Who was your mentor? Who else helped?
- What is the most unusual or controversial finding about your topic? What might be a next step to extend your topic?

Answering Difficult Questions

Give students some tips on how to handle tough questions or questions that they do not know how to answer. Some tips are:

- If you do not understand the question, ask the judges to repeat the question or rephrase the question. This gives you time to think about an answer.
- If a question does not seem to pertain to what you have studied, state that. Indicate that although the question is interesting and related, it is not something you covered in your research.
- If a question is asked that you should know the answer to and do not, indicate that. Also, explain how you would determine an answer.

Exhibition Scoring Guide

Students as well as judges need to be familiar with the scoring guide. Provide exemplars where possible so students know exactly what the expectations are to achieve a high rating. Scoring guides need to be developed for each aspect of the exhibition.

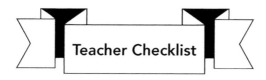

Teacher Checklist

Yes	No	
☐	☐	Students knew what skills and knowledge they would need to demonstrate through the exhibition.
☐	☐	Presentation skills were defined for students.
☐	☐	Students were aware of the various components of a successful presentation.
☐	☐	Students had opportunities to make presentations prior to the exhibition presentation.
☐	☐	Mentors/coaches that had an interest or background in the students' topics were paired with students.
☐	☐	Standards were identified and agreed to by educators and community members.
☐	☐	The various components of the exhibition were clearly understood by students.
☐	☐	The exhibition consisted of a real product with real deadlines for a real audience.
☐	☐	Preparation for the exhibition included instruction in research and analytical skills as well as content.
☐	☐	A coaching aspect was present whereby teachers/mentors coached students toward excellence in their performance.
☐	☐	Scoring guides for the exhibition were developed and understood by students.

Yes	No	
☐	☐	The raters were trained in the use of the scoring guides and the assessment of the exhibition.
☐	☐	Following the exhibitions, students and staff reflected on the results of the exhibition and discussed possible improvements.

APPLICATION

Problem-based Learning

Defining Problems

Problem-based learning (PBL) requires the use of real-world problems. This adds an exciting authenticity for students but creates challenges for you. Real-world problems, by their nature, are messy. It is often difficult to predict how long it will take students to develop a solution. These problems don't match well to traditional classroom resources such as textbooks and exams. PBL using real-world problems demands more preparation and a high degree of comfort with the realization that things will not always go as planned. So be prepared for the unexpected. These cautions aside, the benefits of problem-based learning outweigh the risks.

Problem-based learning is organized around an ill-structured problem that:

- is complex and messy in nature
- has no simple, fixed "right" solution
- requires inquiry, information-gathering, and reflection

Here are some examples of open-ended problems used in PBL:

- You are a scientist at the State Department of Nuclear Safety. Some people in a small community feel their health is at risk because a company keeps thorium piled above ground at one of plants. What action, if any, should be taken?
- You are a consultant to the U.S. Department of Fish and Wildlife. A first draft of a plan for the reintroduction of wolves to Yellowstone National Park has received strong, negative testimony at Senate hearings. What is your advice regarding the plan?
- You are a member of President Truman's Interim Committee. What advice will you give the president to help end the war in the Pacific? An atomic bomb has just been detonated at Los Alamos.

Problem-based Learning Cycle

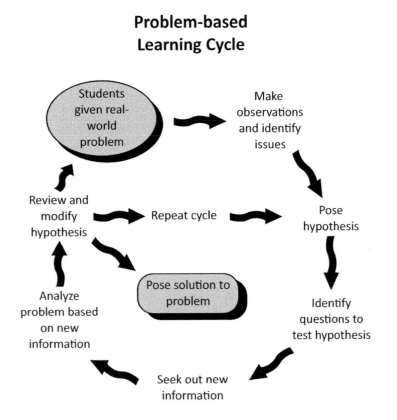

In PBL, the problem comes before anything else. Problems provide clues, context, and motivation; they are the maps that guide learners to useful facts and concepts. Problems should not include detailed information. A "good" problem cannot be understood or resolved at first encounter; it should challenge thinking, require thoughtful research, and demand extensive learning.

The diagram on the previous page illustrates the PBL cycle. After posing an initial hypothesis, students use the learning issues to seek out additional information. This information is used to reexamine the problem. Based on this information, students can modify the existing hypothesis or reject it and repeat the process.

Finding Problems

Problems need to be connected to the curriculum, but efforts should be made to make them real-world and about issues that are related to the students' experiences. Problems are often interdisciplinary, so be prepared when creating a problem in one subject to cross over into other disciplines.

Problems are difficult to design to obtain the proper balance of a well-defined problem with no obvious solution, but with clues that trigger students to pursue in-depth learning. Inspiration for problems can come from newspapers, news reports, literature, state or national policy issues, curriculum guides, technology innovations, social problems, or community issues. Think of controversies, conflicts, debates, dilemmas, political decisions, or complex processes. By examining many of the issues around you, you can identify rich problems for students to analyze.

Once you identify a potential subject, think it through to see if it includes sufficient issues for students to investigate. A good way to analyze the problem is to develop a visual concept map. By mapping out a number of potential issues, you can decide if there are enough topics that relate to the curriculum and will provide good learning opportunities for students.

Teacher's Role

Your role in PBL is divided into three key areas: designer, coach, and evaluator.

In the designer role, you complete the essential creation of an interesting and doable real-world problem. The problem must be one that can be completed with the resources and time available to students. You must also clearly define how the problem relates to the skills and knowledge that have been set for this overall learning experience. PBL may be a waste of time unless it develops the skills that are expected of students.

As students work on the problem, you assume the coaching role. You help shape the students' efforts, reminding them of the problem, keeping them focused on the task, providing clues when they are stuck, and offering encouragement. A good coach remains on the sidelines and lets the students play the game. This applies to coaching problem-based learning as well. Let the students struggle some and develop confidence in their abilities as they work through solutions. A successful solution will be a source of pride only if it is truly their work.

Your role as evaluator is to provide the final determination of the quality of the work. Your expertise in the problem, related skills, and evaluation techniques is essential. In many cases, you do not judge the final work but rather facilitate evaluation by developing scoring guides and/or training peer or external evaluators. Another part of your role as evaluator is to give feedback on progress while students are engaged. This formative type of evaluation helps to improve learning while students are problem solving.

Students assume a different role in PBL in that they are active problemsolvers, decision-makers, and meaning-makers rather than passive listeners.

You model, coach, provide support and encouragement for the beginning investigators and then step aside to observe as students complete their work. Collaboration among students should be encouraged.

Connecting Related Skills

One of the values of PBL is that it demands the use of many different skill areas. Make sure students understand that they will be expected to use and will often be evaluated on language, problem-solving, and inquiry skills as well as knowledge in several disciplines. It is important to structure learning experiences so that they emphasize and reinforce all of the related skills. Avoid the situation where students become so focused on solving the problem that they fail to develop desired skills and knowledge along the way. Well-designed scoring guides and individual coaching will ensure that related academic skills are covered.

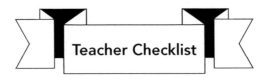

Teacher Checklist

In planning the problem-based learning activity, you:

Yes   No

☐   ☐   Selected or created an appropriate/relevant/compelling problem to use.

☐   ☐   Chose a case/problem that was appropriate to the curriculum objectives and the learners' needs.

☐   ☐   Made the problem as realistic as possible and included appropriate background.

☐   ☐   Gathered information about students' prior experiences and expectations.

☐   ☐   Selected or created appropriate resources to use for presenting the problem.

☐   ☐   Arranged for other resources students will need.

During the problem-based learning, you:

☐   ☐   Helped the students to present their problem in engaging, sequential ways.

☐   ☐   Helped the students to elicit and identify significant facts and generate hypotheses, ideas, and issues.

☐   ☐   Encouraged students to identify and share what they already know.

☐   ☐   Helped students do their own thinking and learning and to identify their learning issues.

Yes   No

☐   ☐   Helped the students decide which learning issues to pursue and how to pursue them.

☐   ☐   Invited reflection on the session's progress and guided planning for the next session.

☐   ☐   Helped the students become increasingly adept at helping each other.

☐   ☐   Helped the students to integrate and apply what they learned.

☐   ☐   Created an environment in which the students felt they could take risks.

☐   ☐   Helped the students to bring closure to the problem in a reasonably timely fashion.

(Adapted from: Westberg, Jane and Jason, Hilliard. *Fostering Learning in Small Groups: A Practical Guide.* New York: Springer Publishing Company, 1996.)

APPLICATION

Project Design

The Design Process

The design process can be used by students, even in early elementary classrooms. It is a four-step process:

1. Start with a problem.
2. Think of a number of ways to solve it.
3. Choose one way.
4. Try it out.

Think of the design process as a loop that circles back to the beginning problem. This reinforces the idea that design solutions can introduce more problems. Later, when students are ready, a more sophisticated eight-step process can be introduced. The process has a number of discrete steps or phases for clarity. In reality students often need to "jump" between steps as their ideas take shape and they develop solutions.

1. Problem
2. Design Brief
3. Investigation
4. Alternative Solutions
5. Best Solution
6. Models and Prototypes
7. Testing and Evaluating
8. Manufacturing (optional)

Problem

A problem is a gap between what is and what someone wants or needs. All problems are not solved with technology designs, but all technology designs arise from a perceived problem. Wherever there are people, there are problems needing solutions. In some cases, the designer may have to invent a product. An example might be a game for blind persons.

At other times the designer may change an existing design. If the handle of a pot becomes too hot to touch, for example, it must be redesigned.

Designers also improve products to make them work even better. Could the chair in the waiting room of a bus or train station be altered so that waiting seems shorter?

Design Brief

A design brief should describe simply and clearly what is to be designed. The design brief cannot be vague. Often there are criteria and constraints, such as how much money can be spent or what materials can be used. An example of a problem and very simple design brief is:

PROBLEM: Blind people cannot play many of the indoor games available to sighted people.

DESIGN BRIEF: Design a game of dominoes that can be played by blind people.

Investigation

The next step is to write down all the information students can think of related to the problem. Consider the following:

- **Function.** A functional object must be designed to solve the problem described in the design brief. The basic question to ask is: "What, exactly, is the use of the object?"

- **Appearance.** How will the object look? The shape, color, and texture should make the object attractive.

- **Materials.** What materials are available to you? You should think about the cost of these materials. Are they affordable? Do they have the right physical properties, such as strength, rigidity, color, and durability?

- **Construction.** Will it be hard to make? Consider what methods you will need to cut, shape, form, join, and finish the material.

- **Safety.** The object you design must be safe to use. It should not cause accidents.

If the project is intended for a specific group of people, then answers may be found by interviewing those people. Of course, students must first discuss the nature of the project with the individual to determine if he/she is willing to be interviewed. Collecting information from people in addition to researching print resources is an excellent way to approach design.

Alternative Solutions

The project design should consider a number of alternative solutions. It is important to write down or draw every idea on paper as it occurs. This will help students to remember and describe them more clearly.

It is easier to discuss a design using illustrations. These first sketches do not have to be detailed or accurate. They should be made quickly. The important thing is to record all ideas. Do not be critical. Try to think of lots of ideas, even some wild ones. The more ideas, the more likely the end solution will be effective.

Designers must keep a careful record of their ideas and progress as they work. There are a number of reasons for this:

- Designers may put aside a project for several months or even years and pick it up again, or the project may be passed along to another group.
- Ideas generated for one project may apply to other projects.
- Designers may want to patent or copyright their work and may need dated records.
- Designers need to protect their ideas in case of intellectual property or liability conflicts.

Therefore, it is critical for the designer to record the thinking, creativity, and problem-solving done in the pursuit of the problem solution.

Students should sketch their designs with as much detail as possible. It is important that students attempt to communicate their ideas neatly in graphical and written forms.

In design projects there is no right answer, only solutions that meet the original design brief with varying degrees of success (positive and negative attributes). A solution may seem excellent, but be too expensive to produce; or a solution may meet all specifications but might create environmental hazards. While these may be extremes, all solutions will have these trade-offs. By generating a number of alternative solutions, the chances of one of those solutions being an appropriate one is increased.

Best Solution

Students may find that they like several of the solutions. Eventually, they must choose one. Usually, careful comparison with the original design brief will help to select the best.

Students should consider:

- their own skills
- the materials available

- time needed to model or build each solution
- the cost of each solution

Deciding among the several possible solutions is not always easy. It helps to summarize the design requirements and solutions and put the summary in a chart. Which would they choose? In cases like this, let it be the one students like best.

Choosing a best solution from the alternatives is a matter of assessing the trade-offs of each design. Which design provides a balance of simplicity, cost-effective to produce and distribute, pleasing aesthetics, and so forth? Students should establish the criteria that they will use to assess the best design solution. Students should be able to defend their choice of direction for their developmental work.

The "best" solution must, of course, meet the criteria established in the design brief and specifications.

Models and Prototypes

A model is a full-size or small-scale simulation of an object. Architects, engineers, and most designers use models.

Models are one more step in communicating an idea. It is far easier to understand an object when seen in three-dimensional form. A scale model is used when designing objects that are large.

A prototype is the first working version of the designer's solution. It is generally full-size and often handmade. For a simple object such as a pencil holder, the designer probably would not make a model. He or she may go directly to a prototype. Before doing so, the designer needs to determine what materials will need to be used to make the device strong enough, durable, pleasing in appearance, etc. Exact dimensions, sizes, etc. are called for at this point.

In most cases, design solutions are modeled in low-cost materials, such as paper, cardboard, foil, etc. Students need to demonstrate the function of their solution idea, but should not be expected to produce a practical, durable product. For example, if movement is an integral part of the design, the model should produce that motion or a simplified motion that demonstrates the "workability" of the design.

Testing and Evaluating

Testing and evaluating answer three basic questions:

1. Does it work?
2. Does it meet the design brief?
3. Will modifications improve the solution?

The question "Does it work?" is basic to good design and must be answered. This same question would be asked by an engineer designing a bridge, by the designer of a subway car, or by an architect planning a new school. If a mistake were made in the final design of the pencil holder, what would happen? The result might simply be unattractive. At worst, the holder would not work well. Not so if a designer makes mistakes in a car's seat belt design in which failure could put someone's life in danger.

How will the project be assessed? In most cases, several ways should be used. In addition to whatever you set as the standard, the students should identify at least one strategy to determine how well their solution meets the criteria outlined in their design brief and specifications. For example, if students were designing a toy for a five-year-old child, they could give the toy to the child and time how long it kept his/her interest, or they could have the toy evaluated by someone who is considered an expert in child development.

While time for every project is limited, it is important to develop and use some kind of evaluation to determine the success of student work.

Students should document evaluation by describing the results of the testing and their own judgment of how well the solution achieved the original goal. In addition, a paragraph or two describing how well they performed in solving the problem should also be a part of any project evaluation. A few sentences should indicate what they would change if they had to redesign their solution, and why.

Manufacturing (optional)

Sometimes the project will involve a product that students can mass-produce. Once everyone is satisfied with the design, students must decide how many to make. Products may be mass-produced in low volume or high volume.

The task of making the product is often divided into pieces. As each piece of the process is completed the product takes shape. Mass production is used to create a quantity of one design. Specialty manufacturing is used to create more customized products.

From the biggest project to the smallest, designers never work alone. But coming together with others to create a workable solution to a problem takes thought and practice. By learning how to work with others through design projects, students acquire skills that transfer to the real world.

Tips for Success

- Choose the elements of project design that make sense for your curriculum.
- Projects take time. Be sure there is adequate time for students to complete the projects. Unfinished work creates frustrations.
- Begin simply and slowly. Don't try anything too complex until you and your students are ready.
- Do what's comfortable for you. Don't try to do it all at once.
- Give students time to learn and practice skills crucial to success: public speaking, listening, planning, resourcefulness, collaborations, cooperation, and personal responsibility.
- Generate group decision-making processes (consensus, majority rule, conflict management) and an understanding of when to apply them.
- The design process is not just focused on a product; documentation is necessary to evaluate the progress of student understanding. Students document their thinking by keeping a record of both the creative and analytical steps in the design process.

- Make sure materials and resources are available. However, don't let limited materials deter you from tackling design projects. Sometimes the best learning comes from designing projects within severe resource constraints.

- Don't forget that taking calculated risks is an important part of good teaching practice. Students may surprise you with their creative talents and thinking ability.

- Project design shouldn't be yet another thing to fit into your already crowded program. Use it to integrate and pull together several standards.

- Before, during, and after a project, remind students about the skills and knowledge they are learning. Too often the project becomes the description of what is learned. Students should be told about the skills and knowledge that will be learned from the project design activity.

- Keep administrators informed of your progress along the way and encourage students to give presentations to administrators and others.

- Use the projects to make greater connections with the community. Keep people informed. Invite parents to help with projects.

- Keep documentation (photos, artwork, writing, videotapes) of project work to share and review.

- Encourage the use of models and pictures to develop and communicate student designs.

- When designing, have students recognize that their designs will have to satisfy multiple requirements. Encourage students to consider as many alternatives as possible. Don't let them "settle" for the first solution.

- When designing, students should gather information independently and use it to help generate a number of ideas. They must recognize that consumers have views and preferences and begin to take them into account.

- Encourage students to express their ideas through the design process. They clarify their ideas through discussion, drawing, and modeling and using their knowledge and understanding.

Teacher Checklist

Yes   No

☐   ☐   The design project was drawn from real people and real needs.

☐   ☐   The design project incorporated skills that relate directly to standards.

☐   ☐   The design process started with a problem.

☐   ☐   The design project was completed by students working in small groups.

☐   ☐   Student groups were heterogeneous (varied learning styles, academic abilities, leadership skills, etc.).

☐   ☐   Student behavioral expectations, rules, and guidelines were set ahead of time.

☐   ☐   A multistep process was followed in project design.

☐   ☐   The students kept journals or wrote about the design process both to document their work and to record their ideas as they went through the design process.

☐   ☐   Criteria for assessment and evaluation of the project were set ahead of time.

☐   ☐   The physical classroom arrangement supports group work and the project design process.

☐   ☐   Students were given opportunities to reflect on ways to improve their project designs.

☐   ☐   Final projects were put on display to showcase student work.

APPLICATION

Research

Four Types of Research

There are several different types of research. One way to categorize research is using a model based on the source and type of information being researched. The diagram below presents a model of four types of research: scientific, analytical, social and descriptive.

Student research focuses on two sources of information. *Primary* information sources are those the student collects directly and uniquely in original form, such as interviews, original documents or experimentation. *Secondary* sources are the collection of information from other research work including publications, library resources and the Internet. The other distinguishing characteristic of research is whether the information is primarily quantitative or qualitative.

Types of Student Research

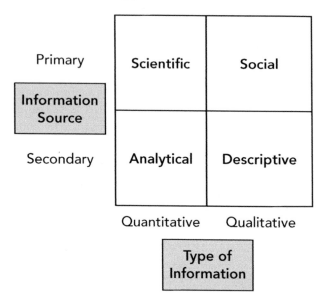

Scientific Research

Scientific research attempts to describe cause-and-effect relationships. Scientific research uses quantitative data from primary information sources. Here, the methodology identifies variables or factors that will have an impact upon the outcome of the research. A variable is changed in some way in order to observe its effect. Scientific research often uses an experimental group and a control group. The control group is as similar as possible to the experimental group of subjects except that the experimental group is receiving some form of special treatment, which is identified as the variable.

Analytical Research

Analytical research attempts to describe things in a systematic, quantitative, and detailed manner. Analytical research uses quantitative data from secondary information sources. Analytical research is typically driven by a need to know something to solve a problem or plan a new activity. When confronting any problem, a logical question is, "How have others done this?" or "What are our possible workable solutions?" Analytical research is a process to look at answers to these questions systematically.

Social Research

Social research examines people's attitudes and opinions. Social research uses qualitative data from primary information sources. Research work is done through the use of surveys of a sampling of a group of people. In social research it is often not possible to create experimental and control groups. Instead, the research compares results of several groups of people to report findings.

Descriptive Research

Descriptive research analyzes existing data into a summary report for a specific purpose. It uses qualitative data from secondary information sources. Descriptive research is the type of research most often done in school. Students examine several information sources to synthesize into a concise report that describes a specific topic. Descriptive research is driven by a topic and the motivation of the researcher rather than by the desire to solve a problem or make an observation.

Following are the steps in each type of research.

Scientific Research

- Make Initial Observation
- Gather Information
- Clarify the Purpose of the Project
- Identify Variables
- Make Hypothesis
- Design Experiments to Test Hypothesis
- Do the Experiments and Record Data

- Record Observations
- Summarize Results
- Draw Conclusions

Analytical Research

- Identify a Topic
- Clarify Needs to be Addressed
- Gather Information
- Interpret Data
- Share Research Findings

Social Research

- Make Initial Observation of Behavior
- Gather Information
- Clarify the Purpose of the Project
- Make Hypothesis
- Design Survey Instruments
- Collect Data
- Summarize Results
- Draw Conclusions

Descriptive Research

- Identify and Develop the Topic
- Find Background Information
- Find Print Resources
- Find Internet Resources
- Evaluate Information Resources
- Cite Resources Using a Standard Format
- Write Descriptive Report

Doing the Research

Suggestions for Using the Internet

Keep Bookmarks. Students should keep their own set of bookmarks. There are several ways this can be accomplished. A central computer, for example, can be set up with folders in the bookmark list for each student.

Keep Students Focused. When students go online to do research, they should have a goal. This will keep them on track as they search. If students are doing general research, they can also start from one of the "student friendly" searching pages or menus on the Internet.

Use Search Engines. Make sure that students know what search engines are available and how to use them. Learning how to search online is not an easy task, but you can get some terrific guidance from the Internet itself.

Custom-Made Web Pages. You can keep students focused when they do research by giving them a particular web page from which to begin their exploration. This web page can be made ahead of time by a teacher or by a team of students who may have already covered this content. If students build content-based web pages as they do this type of research, you will end up with your own bank of content-based web pages. If you or your students don't know how to make web pages, you can use different sets of bookmarks to accomplish the same goals.

Reliability of Web Pages. One of the challenges is evaluating websites for reliability and biases. There are a number of pages that offer checklists or rubrics to help users.

Citing Electronic Resources

Just as students need to cite the books and periodicals they use to support their research, they must also cite online sources of information. Classroom Connect developed the following method to help students cite Internet resources as accessed through their Internet browsers. This method makes it easy for you to check the veracity of every online source your students cite. Also included below is information specifying how to cite the graphics, sounds, and video clips students retrieve for use in their multimedia presentations. (Source: Classroom Connect, www.connectedteacher.com/newsletter/citeintres.asp, August 30, 2012)

E-mail

Structure: Author of e-mail message. *Subject line of the message.* E-mail: recipient from author, date of document or download.

Example: Daggett, Willard R. *Rigorous and Relevant Learning.* E-mail: rrteacher@aol.com from daggettwr@aol.com, August 30, 2012.

Websites

Structure: Author. *Title of item.* URL, date of document or download.

Example: International Center for Leadership in Education. *Staff Development.* www.daggett.com/staff.htm/, August 30, 2012.

Online Images, Sounds, Video Clips

Structure: Description or title of multimedia. [Online image], URL, date of document, image, or download.

Example: *International Center Logo.* [Online image], www.daggett. com/_borders/copy_of_icle1.gif, August 30, 2012.

Teaching Students How to Use the Library

By far the most effective way to help students become more proficient in using library resources is to integrate library use with a research project. Use the following suggestions to instruct students on use of the library.

- Assume that students have minimal knowledge of library resources and research techniques.
- Keep things simple, yet offer a variety or breadth in options.
- Review available library resources to avoid creating a "mob scene," with too many students chasing too few books or articles.

- Provide clear examples, with everything in writing.
- Devote a class period to a presentation by a librarian.
- Bring the class to the library for a guided tour. This offers the students an opportunity to ask questions about specific resources in context, but doesn't teach much about research strategies or evaluation of resources.

Characteristics of a Good Topic

Good research starts with a sound topic. The following criteria will help you work with students to select good topics.

- The topic is interesting to the student. Reading research the student finds boring will make the task much harder.
- The topic is appropriate for the course in which you are doing the project. Just because a student is interested in motorcycles does not mean this is an appropriate research topic for your class.
- The topic is researchable. That is, the student can locate and obtain references on the topic despite limited information sources.
- The topic is narrow. Whenever possible, help students limit the scope of the topic by focusing on a selected population (e.g., age group, species), a particular theory, a singular methodology, or the type of materials used (e.g., verbal, pictorial, etc.). A topic that is too broad will leave the student feeling overwhelmed by the amount of material to be reviewed.

Not All Student Research Is Created Equal

There can be several different educational objectives for using student research as an instructional strategy. You need to be clear as to the objectives you are trying to develop through the research. The criteria for evaluating the research should emphasize the following important objectives.

Detailed Knowledge of a Topic. Often research is assigned as a way for students or a class to learn more detailed information about a topic.

In these instances, it is important to stress the quantity of the description presented. Quality of writing and presentation may be of lesser importance.

Writing and Presenting. When the important objective is the way the research results are presented, you may give greater weight to the quality of the writing and presentation.

Original Research. If the emphasis is on student observations and research skills, be sure to focus on the development of the hypothesis and collection of primary source data.

Data Manipulation. Often, the goal is to strengthen students' ability to work with data. They do not need original data to do this and might have complex tasks in an analytical project to manipulate, analyze, interpret, and present data.

Use of Information Systems. If the emphasis is on the use of information sources such as the library or Internet, it matters less that students select a good topic or have a focused hypothesis. The emphasis should be on how well students acquired information using these systems.

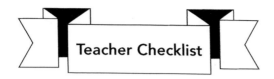

Teacher Checklist

Planning Research

Yes   No

☐   ☐   Students understand different types of research and the purpose of the research project.

☐   ☐   Research projects are appropriately challenging to the developmental level of the students.

☐   ☐   Research projects include an authentic component, such as an interview or personal connection, making it more difficult to plagiarize Internet-available reports.

☐   ☐   Students are encouraged to make thoughtful observations and develop these observations into researchable topics.

☐   ☐   Students select a topic that is appropriate, interesting, not too broad, and not one with which they are too familiar.

☐   ☐   Research topics relate to course objectives and standards.

☐   ☐   Students are able to adapt a research topic to their personal interests.

☐   ☐   Students are encouraged to use primary information sources as much as possible.

Facilitating Student Research

☐   ☐   Students have access to and skills in using library information sources.

☐   ☐   Students have access to and skills in using Internet information sources.

Yes   No

☐   ☐   Younger students have circumscribed access to Internet resources in order to prevent accessing undesirable material.

☐   ☐   All students have equal access to material, tools, and opportunity to complete research reports.

☐   ☐   Specific deadlines are established for students.

☐   ☐   Throughout the research process, students are encouraged and coached to ensure they are "on task" and meeting expectations.

Evaluating Student Reports and Presentations

☐   ☐   A detailed scoring guide is used.

☐   ☐   The evaluation emphasizes the objectives that relate to the course.

☐   ☐   Students know the evaluation criteria in advance.

Simulation/ Role-playing

Uses for Simulation

Simulations can be used for various phases of instruction: presentation, guidance, practice, and assessment. This makes simulations one of the most versatile types of instructional strategy. Simulations can be used: before the formal presentation of new material to spark student interest; to help students recall previous knowledge about the topic; and to provide a concrete example. After students have been introduced to new content, simulations can be used to enable them to transfer what they have learned to an actual application.

Simulations can be used in a variety of instructional activities. These can extend from the simple introductory exercise to culminating activities that include extensive student research and preparation. Some examples are described below.

Icebreakers. Simulations are effective for team building and introducing course content. They also serve as a means of introducing students to a learning environment that encourages participation and interaction. These types of simulations should be short, creative, and focus on communication skills. An example is "Detective Story," developed by Ken Jones (1991). In this simulation, students become ideas for characters in an unfinished detective story still in the author's imagination. The author has a writer's block that disallows the ideas coming together. In pairs, the students must meet and negotiate ideas to try to get the story to unfold.

Developing Empathy and Understanding. Numerous simulations bring students into situations in which they need to make critical choices and deal with diversity and social conflict. These real-life experiences broaden students' perspectives and assist in developing greater sensitivity, understanding, and tolerance of differing social, cultural, economic, and political aspects of society. In *Simulations: A Sourcebook for Teachers and Trainers*, Jones describes "Tenement," a British simulation that engages students in the problems and challenges of living in a large-city tenement. Students assume various roles of tenement life, such as landlord, tenant, and representative from a public agency. Through the simulation, students become aware of a lifestyle that might otherwise be foreign to them. Awareness is enhanced by learning ways to solve some of the problems associated with tenement dwelling.

Analyze Social Problems. It is possible through simulations to immerse students in the causes, effects, and scope of social problems. Students determine their impact or consequences and analyze prescribed solutions. The tenement example is also appropriate for students to look closer at social problems and possible solutions.

Explore the Future. Computer simulations allow students to predict or explore the future. Students practice creative problem solving and build capacity to manage and cope with continuous change as they make decisions about future ideas, events, etc. The future of a city is the subject of a commercial simulation, "Cities." Students make choices about the future life and activities of a city. (Lewis, 1974)

Develop Analytical and Research Skills. Typically, simulations enhance students' ability to analyze situations. Simulations also nurture the ability to transfer and apply analytical and research skills to other curricular areas.

Develop Oral and Written Communication Skills. Involvement in simulations requires students to analyze, evaluate, and extrapolate ideas. These activities stimulate communication skills. Students learn to negotiate; argue; interview; take notes; draft, edit, and organize; speak publicly; and listen. A common simulation involves students assuming roles as representatives of other countries in a United Nations debate over a topic of current economic, social, or political interest. In these roles, students strengthen their communication skills through negotiating and debating.

Factors to Consider When Selecting a Simulation

1. The simulation must match the instructional objective.

2. The purpose of the simulation must always relate to the course content and competencies. Assigning simulations because students enjoy them is not a good reason to use this strategy.

3. Placement of the simulation in a course is a consideration. There are distinct advantages to having the simulation at the beginning or the end of the course. At the beginning, the simulation will encourage interaction and participation. At the end, the simulation may be a culminating or summative activity. Sufficient time needs to be provided not only to complete the simulation but also to discuss it.

4. Time for simulations is a factor in planning your instruction. Your experience with using simulations will to some extent determine how much time you allow for them. As you are introducing simulations, keep them brief. Use one class period or an extended class. After you become more experienced at facilitating simulations, you can incorporate ones that require more time to complete.

5. Participation is a key component of simulations. Try to use ones that involve many students. In most cases, the simulation will indicate the ideal number of participants. Various roles can be modified or extended to increase participation. Avoid using simulations that engage only a few students.

6. Careful consideration needs to be given to role assignments. The consequences of these in relation to the success of the simulation need to be addressed. The process of assigning or designating roles can lead to other perceptions unrelated to the simulation. This may be particularly true in the assignment of high status roles.

7. Many simulations require teams. Thus, you need to assist students in developing teaming skills and strategies and provide them with opportunities to function effectively as a team. Capitalize on class groupings that are already in place.

8. Debriefing activities need to be student-centered. Students should debrief using a guide that you develop on the major outcomes of the simulation and additional learning resulting from the simulation.

9. Identify all the resources you need to implement the simulation. Preview materials and itemize what will be needed to have success.

Implementing the Simulation

In order to maximize student learning from the simulation, decisions about organization and grading need to be made prior to implementing the simulation.

1. Be familiar with the simulation. Know its objectives, procedures, etc., and be prepared to introduce, conduct, and process it. Plan all pre-simulation activities, such as materials, instruction sheets, seating arrangements, etc.

2. Determine your role. Are you an observer or a guide? It is necessary to monitor the simulation but only in a facilitating manner. It is the students' learning opportunity so you need to be careful not to intervene unnecessarily. You are not an active participant. Rather, provide help as needed.

3. Assess performance in the simulation. Whether and how the simulation is to be graded needs to be decided prior to the simulation. Care must be taken to ensure that grading does not interfere with students' risk-taking, interaction, outcomes, and other

behaviors. An alternative to grading the simulation is to grade the planning phase or post-simulation analysis/debriefing.

During the simulation, you can base the assessment of students' behavior on a number of factors, such as level of interaction, communication skills, teaming skills; and of course, on what students have mastered or assimilated. What have students learned from the simulation exercise? Students need to be well aware ahead of time as to how they are being assessed.

4. Consider grouping carefully. Divide students into as many small groups as possible. Interaction may decrease significantly if the group is too large, particularly at the secondary level. Heterogeneous groups have proven more successful than homogeneous groups; students are more motivated in heterogeneous groups.

5. Allow enough instructional time. If there are time limits, particularly in games, advise students of these and provide deadline warnings. Schedule the simulation(s) at the most appropriate time during the course.

6. Determine the educational value of the simulation. Debriefing questions, which are usually included in the simulation, are effective in measuring the simulation's success in meeting the instructional objective. In *Simulations: A Sourcebook for Teachers and Trainers*, Jones suggests that the teacher lead a discussion first on any problems students encountered and how they solved them. Some general questions for discussion are:

- How did the group organize itself?
- Was the organization effective?
- What alternatives were suggested?
- Did the group or individuals explore the options, analyze the situation, and plan accordingly?
- How effective was the communication?
- What did students learn?
- How would students act differently if they were in a similar situation in the future?
- What did students learn that could be transferred to other situations?

Designing a Simulation

When first using simulations, it is best to start with commercially developed products. However, after you become more proficient with this instructional strategy, you may prefer to develop your own simulated activities based on the course content and competencies.

To design a simulation, use the following points as guides:

1. Identify the educational objective. Determine the simulation's purpose and define each concept and competency you wish to develop.

2. Define the model to be replicated. Decide what problem or subject will be the focus of the simulation activity. Outline the scenario and determine the purpose and name of the organization involved, nature and number of roles, etc.

3. Explain the dynamics of the model. Describe roles for both students and teacher; outline types of interactions that will occur. Define the behaviors on which the simulation is focusing.

4. Outline the rules of participation. Define procedural and behavioral rules as well as the goal and how students will be motivated. Establish how feedback will be given and evaluation carried out. Set standards for measurement of goal attainment and develop a process for resolving conflicts and enforcing rules.

5. Prepare discussion questions for debriefing.

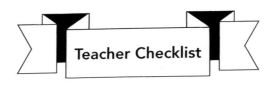

Teacher Checklist

Yes   No

☐   ☐   Students learned from what they do rather than what they were told, observed, or read.

☐   ☐   The activity involved real-world problem-solving experiences and reflected reality.

☐   ☐   The simulation's instructional objective was clear.

☐   ☐   Financial and classroom resources needed for the simulation were identified.

☐   ☐   During the simulation, it was safe for students to make mistakes.

☐   ☐   Students received immediate feedback on their progress.

☐   ☐   Learning was active rather than passive; everyone participated.

☐   ☐   Students, not you, were the "main players."

☐   ☐   Group composition was appropriate to the simulation and supported interaction.

☐   ☐   A debriefing process was carefully planned and carried out.

☐   ☐   There was a rubric for assessing students' behavior during the simulation.

☐   ☐   Students were aware of the grading process.

Socratic Seminar

Elements of Socratic Seminar

A Socratic Seminar fosters active learning as participants explore and evaluate the ideas, issues, and values in a particular text. A seminar begins with an open-ended question to start students reflecting on the meaning of the text. Through careful use of listening techniques and further questions, the teacher as facilitator leads the students to deeper reflection on the work in question. A seminar consists of four inter-dependent elements: (1) the text being considered, (2) the questions raised, (3) the seminar leader, and (4) the participants. A closer look at each of these elements helps explain the unique character of a Socratic Seminar.

The Text

Socratic Seminar texts are chosen for their richness in ideas, issues, and values and their ability to stimulate extended, thoughtful dialogue. The text can be drawn from readings in literature, history, science, math, health, and philosophy or from works of art or music. A good text raises important questions in the participants' minds, questions for which there are no right or wrong answers. At the end of a successful Socratic Seminar, participants often leave with more questions than they started with.

The Question

A Socratic Seminar opens with a question, either posed by the leader or solicited from participants as they acquire more experience in seminars. An opening question has no right answer; instead it reflects a genuine curiosity on the part of the questioner. A good opening question leads participants back to the text as they speculate, evaluate, define, and clarify the issues involved. Responses to the opening question generate new questions from the leader and participants, leading to new responses. In this way, the line of inquiry in a Socratic Seminar evolves on the spot rather than being predetermined by the leader.

The Leader

In a Socratic Seminar, the leader plays dual roles as leader and participant. The seminar leader consciously demonstrates habits of mind that lead to a thoughtful exploration of the ideas in the text by keeping the discussion focused on the text, asking follow-up questions, helping participants clarify their positions when arguments become confused, and involving reluctant participants while restraining their more vocal peers.

As a seminar participant, the leader actively engages in the group's exploration of the text. To do this effectively, the leader must know the text well enough to anticipate varied interpretations and recognize important possibilities in each. The leader must also be patient enough to allow participants' understandings to evolve and be willing to help participants explore nontraditional insights and unexpected interpretations. Assuming this dual role of leader and participant is easier if the opening question is one that truly interests the leader as well as the participants.

The Participants

In a Socratic Seminar, participants share with the leader the responsibility for the quality of the seminar. Good seminars occur when participants study the text closely in advance, listen actively, share their ideas and questions in response to the ideas and questions of others, and search for evidence in the text to support their ideas.

Participants acquire good seminar behaviors through participating in seminars and reflecting on them afterward. After each seminar, the leader and participants discuss the experience and identify ways of improving the next seminar. Before each new seminar, the leader offers coaching and practice in specific habits of mind that improve reading, thinking, and discussing. Eventually, when participants realize that the leader is not looking for right answers but is encouraging them to think out loud and to exchange ideas openly, they discover the excitement of exploring important issues through shared inquiry. This excitement creates willing participants, eager to examine ideas in a rigorous, thoughtful manner.

Room Arrangement

Modification of room arrangements is often necessary. It is very important that the students have direct eye contact with one another and that they appear equal to the discussion leader. This is most often done by arranging the desks in a circle, with the teacher sitting at one of the desks. A seminar is probably ideal with 15–20 students, although it can work with 25–30. If the classroom is not large enough to arrange all of the desks in a circle, create two circles, one inside the other. The inner circle is the seminar group and the outer circle observes. To maintain the interest of students in the outer circle, leave two seats in the inner circle empty. As the seminar proceeds, when a person in the outer circle wishes to add a comment, he or she moves from the outer circle to take a seat temporarily in the inner circle.

Conducting a Socratic Seminar

Preparation

- Read the assigned text carefully. Focus on formulating provocative questions while you're reading. Select short passages for special attention.

- At the start of each seminar, your role is to get the discussion moving by setting the stage. A few brief comments are in order; but remember, you're not there to deliver a lecture.

- Choose an introductory question in advance that is broad, open-ended, and provocative.

- Set the room arrangement in a circle to support a positive environment for a seminar.

Conducting a Seminar

- Listen carefully so that you can follow every answer with another question.

- Stick with the subject at hand, and encourage the group to turn to the assigned texts frequently to support their ideas. Do not let the discussion wander or participants ramble.

- Use neither praise nor negative comments. Your role is to press participants to clarify and amplify their ideas.

- Insist on standards of intellectual rigor. A good seminar is focused.

- Remember that your role is to be a co-learner and discussion facilitator, not an authority on "correct" thinking.

- At the end of the seminar, give the group time for thoughts on how the discussion evolved. Ask each individual to reflect. Use the feedback to guide future meetings.

Guidelines for Participants

- Do not participate if you are not prepared. A seminar should not be a bull session. Read the assigned text(s) thoroughly and reflectively.

- Mark key issues or take notes on the text to make it easier to refer to citations during the seminar.

- Refer to the text when needed during the discussion. A seminar is not a test of memory. You are not "learning a subject." Your goal is to understand the ideas, issues, and values reflected in the text.

- Form opinions you can defend by citing evidence in the text.

- If you do not understand something, ask for clarification.

- Stick to the point currently under discussion; make notes about ideas you want to come back to.

- Search for connections with previous reading and other discussions.

- Listen carefully and completely to another's opinion before forming a response.

- Listen critically to others and take issue with inaccuracies or illogical reasoning.

- Maintain an open mind to a diversity of opinions.

- Speak up so that all can hear you.

- Be courteous and respectful of peers.

- It's OK to "pass" when asked to contribute.

- Avoid repeating the comments made by others.

- Talk to fellow students not just to the leader or teacher.

- Discuss ideas rather than each other's opinions.

Teacher Checklist

Participants

Yes No

☐ ☐ Have read and analyzed the text.

☐ ☐ Speak loudly and clearly and avoid inappropriate language.

☐ ☐ Listen to others respectfully and support each other.

☐ ☐ Cite reasons and evidence for their statements.

☐ ☐ Talk to each other, not just to you.

☐ ☐ Question others in a civil manner.

Leader

☐ ☐ Reminds students of the rules for a Socratic Seminar.

☐ ☐ Sits at the same level as the students.

☐ ☐ Gets all participants engaged early.

☐ ☐ States a clear opening question.

☐ ☐ Corrects misunderstandings without demeaning students.

☐ ☐ Allows for discussion of disagreements.

☐ ☐ Listens carefully to participants' statements.

☐ ☐ Accepts participants' answers without judgment.

☐ ☐ Serves as a good model of seminar participation.

Yes   No

☐   ☐   Speaks infrequently so that students can carry the conversation.

☐   ☐   Allows time (pauses) for thinking.

☐   ☐   Brings the seminar to closure and reinforces major points made.

☐   ☐   Conducts a reflection session for feedback from students.

APPLICATION

Teacher Questions

Types of Questions

In order to ask the appropriate questions at the right times, it is important to understand the different types of questions and the kinds of information/response which they elicit. Questions can be grouped into six major types based upon the purpose in teaching and learning:

1. Information
2. Analytical
3. Imaginative
4. Follow-up
5. Opinion
6. Conversational

In the context of teaching and learning, information questions, analytical questions and imaginative questions pose the greatest potential for creating learning conversations. By using such questions, the teacher can stimulate thoughtful student reflection and learning.

Teacher questions can be a useful strategy in many aspect of teaching to:

- Increase student engagement in learning.
- Enhance the quality and depth of student thinking.
- Develop a questioning attitude in students whereby they learn to ask questions and seek answers.

Information Questions

Information questions are requests for specific information and have a narrow range of response. They are sometimes called "closed-ended questions" because there are limited responses. Such questions include, "What year was the Declaration of Independence signed?" and "What is the square of 8?" Close-ended questions are precise probes for specific information and a quick response.

There are many group instruction situations where closed-ended information questions are appropriate. When seeking a simple recall of information, use a straightforward request for an answer. Closed-ended questions also are easier for students to answer than open-ended questions and can be used to build their confidence and willingness to respond prior to introducing questions that require more complex thinking.

Analytical Questions

Analytical questions serve as stimulants to students to reflect and compare information and then to form a response. Analytical questions and imaginative questions are the two types of open-ended questions where there are multiple appropriate responses to a question, or there may be no obvious answer at all.

For an analytical question, students must consider a wide range of information. This type of open-ended question attempts to create convergent thinking to bring large amounts of information to a logical response. Examples of analytical questions are: "What factors contributed to the American Revolution?" and "What were the reasons for space exploration?" This type of question requires more reflection in response.

There are several types of open-ended analytical questions that teachers can use to stimulate learning. When attempting to create thoughtful responses, it is important to be sure that the questions cannot be answered with a single fact or other simple response. Some ambiguity is appropriate, but the questions themselves should be precise enough to be understandable and should relate clearly to the topic under consideration.

Following are three types of analytical questions that can serve as guides when thinking of good questions to enhance learning.

Explanation questions encourage students to think about a process or system. By having to describe processes in their own terms, teachers can reinforce students' perspectives on the essence of learning and require them to confront their own understanding of the topic.

Discovery questions require students to figure something out and examine an idea from different vantage points. These questions should present interesting problems that do not have simple or obvious solutions. They also should require students to link previously acquired information with new information.

Causation questions require students to think about possible reasons why something occurred. This type of question is ideal for making connections between human behavior and its consequences or for investigating scientific phenomena in nature.

Imaginative Questions

Imaginative questions are the second type of open-ended questions where students are challenged to consider vast amounts of information and where there are multiple correct responses. In this case, instead of stimulating convergent thinking to analyze information, the intent is to create divergent thinking and stimulate new combinations of information. Students are expected to create novel and unique responses to imaginative questions. Examples of imaginative questions are: "How could we count quantities if there were no numbers 6–10?" and "What would America be like if the British had been victorious in the American Revolution?"

Imaginative questions stimulate student thinking and lead to deeper understanding of an idea or concept. Imaginative questions can be divided into two subcategories: hypothetical and creative. In each case, students are expected think through responses that are novel or unique.

Hypothetical questions pose new situations and require students to look at topics in different ways. Rather than just recalling the facts of a lesson or other events in the class, students must link instruction to other background experiences.

Creative questions require students to design unique solutions from their own perspective. Students apply what they know about a situation to create an appropriate solution to a complex problem.

Follow-Up Questions

An important aspect of teacher questions is handling student responses. Follow-up questions are those questions teachers ask following the initial student response to probe for further information, clarify misunderstandings, or redirect thinking. These questions directly relate to the initial question and are based on student responses. Examples of these questions are: "Why do you think that happened?" or "Is that the only factor?"

Depending on whether or not the student response is on target, the teacher can use one of several follow-up strategies to reinforce, probe, refocus, or redirect. If the students do not respond, use either a rephrase or redirect strategy.

Probe questions are useful if the initial student response is superficial. Probing questions make students explore their first reactions. Probes are useful to get students more involved in analyzing their own and other students' ideas. Probes can be used to: analyze a student's statement, make a student aware of underlying assumptions, or justify or evaluate a statement.

Refocus questions are appropriate when a student provides a response that appears out of context. The teacher can ask a refocus question to encourage the student to tie his or her response to the content being discussed. This technique is also used to shift attention to a new topic.

Redirect questions ask one student to comment on another student's response, thus redirecting the conversation. One purpose of using this technique is to encourage more students to participate. This strategy can also be used to allow a student to correct another student's incorrect statement or to respond to another student's question.

Rephrasing questions are used when a student provides an incorrect response or no response. Instead of telling the student he or she is incorrect or calling upon another student, the teacher can try to reword the question to make it clearer, provide a clue, or break the question into easier parts.

Opinion Questions

Opinion questions are often not intended to probe for information, but are a way for the questioner to make known his or her own opinions. Such questions could be "Do you really believe that garbage?" or "Why does she act that way?" Opinion questions seek no real information, and often lead the person being questioned to give a predetermined response. This includes the typical rhetorical question that comes to mind in troubling personal experiences and has no answer, "Why me?"

Conversational Questions

Conversational questions are simple prompts used to facilitate conversation. The actual response is often less important than the fact that a response is made. Some examples of this type of question include such everyday expressions as "How are you?," "Isn't it a nice day?," and "Are you listening to me?" These questions are used to start or redirect a conversation.

Effective Use of Information Questions

Information questions typically begin with "who," "what," "when," or "where." Examples: "Who was the first person to land on the moon?" "What is the first step in the writing process?" "When did Columbus visit America?" or "Where is the Mississippi River?"

Effective Use of Analytical Questions

Explanation questions ask students to think about a process or system. Explanation questions usually start with *How do . . . ?* Examples:

- How do you find the midpoint of a triangle?
- How do you determine the mass of an object?
- How does supply and demand affect prices of commodities?
- How does our government create new laws?

Discovery questions require students to figure something out and examine an idea from different vantage points. Discovery questions usually start with *What is . . . ?* Examples:

- What is the central theme of the story?
- What is the relationship between the number of sides of an object and the total degrees in all of the angles?
- What are examples of simple machines around the house?
- What is the meaning of the metaphor in the reading passage?

Causation questions require students to think about possible causes why something occurred. Causation questions usually start with *Why . . . ?* Examples:

- Why did America enter the war in 1941?
- Why do compounds dissolve faster at higher temperatures?
- Why did 15th-century explorers travel the world?
- Why do some objects float in water?
- Why does lightning occur in thunderstorms?

Effective Use of Imaginative Questions

Hypothetical questions pose new situations to students and require them to look at topics in different ways. Hypothetical questions usually ask *"What"* or *"How"* and begin with a conditional clause that starts with *"If . . . "* Examples:

- If a car had no speedometer, how would you measure speed?
- If you could go back in time to the era of the dinosaurs, how would you describe the world so we would know about it today?
- If you created your own language, what would you use for an alphabet?
- If Earth took 100 hours to rotate around its axis, what would be different?

Creative questions require students to design unique solutions from their own perspective. Creative questions usually start with *How would you . . . ?* Examples:

- How would you protect an endangered species of fish in a local lake?
- How would you divide a round pizza in seven equal pieces?
- How would you measure the height of a tall building?
- How would you measure the distance between two cities?
- How would you create a government where everyone had a chance to voice opinions on the issues?

Effective Use of Follow-up Questions

Even before asking follow-up questions, good instructional technique requires positive reinforcement of good student responses in order to encourage future participation. You can reinforce by making positive statements and by using positive nonverbal communication. Positive nonverbal responses include smiling, nodding, and maintaining eye contact, while negative nonverbal responses include appearing distracted by looking at notes or at the board while students speak, or by shuffling papers.

It is a good idea to vary reinforcement techniques using several verbal statements and nonverbal reactions. Try not to overuse positive reinforcement in the classroom by giving high praise to every comment. Students begin to question the sincerity of reinforcement if every response is given equal positive reinforcement.

Probe questions make students explore initial comments. Examples:

- What else can you tell me?
- What is an example of that concept?
- What do you mean?
- Why do you think that happened?

Refocus questions encourage the student to tie his or her response to the content being discussed. Examples:

- How does that relate to what we saw?
- Is there a connection to the other causes?
- Is there another reason?

Redirect questions ask one student to comment on another student's response. Examples:

- Maria, do you agree with Mark's explanation?
- Derek, from your experience, does what Markita said seem true?
- Jeff, can you give me an example of the concept that Luis mentioned?

Rephrasing questions try to reword the teacher question to make it clearer, provide a clue, or break it into easier parts. Examples:

- Initial question: How does the Bill of Rights protect individual freedoms?

  Rephrased question: What are examples of personal freedoms mentioned in the Bill of Rights?

- Initial question: What is an ecosystem?

  Rephrased question : What are examples of plants and animals that need each other to survive?

- Initial question: What is the name of an eight-sided shape?

  Rephrased question: What names do you know for multi-sided shapes?

General Suggestions

Do Planning with Other Teachers to Create a Good List of Questions

Don't just wing it with questions that pop into your head at the spur of the moment. If you want to stimulate good quality thinking with your students, plan thoughtful questions. In a group, brainstorm several possible questions and discuss those that will be the most effective. Share questions that work well, and keep a record of those good questions for future use.

Compliment Students

Questions are part of creating a conversation. When used in a conversation, you should compliment students on their response. Don't routinely praise all comments, but praise students when they do contribute and compliment particularly good responses. By effectively using praise, you can stimulate more student thought and response to questions.

Give Time for Students to Think

Don't expect an immediate response. Frequently having students think on their own and discuss their ideas in groups of two or three will enable them to think through ideas before responding in front of the class.

Wait 3–5 Seconds

One factor that can have powerful effects on student participation is the amount of time you wait between asking a question and doing something else (calling on a student or rewording the question). Research on classroom questioning and information processing indicates that students need at least three seconds to comprehend a question, consider the available information, formulate an answer, and begin to respond. In contrast, the same research established that on average, a classroom teacher allows less than one second of wait-time. Allow three to five seconds of wait-time following questions. Simpler questions require less wait-time, perhaps only three seconds. Complex questions may require five seconds or more. With particularly complex questions, tell students to spend two or three minutes considering the question and writing down some ideas.

Listen to the Student

This helps to focus the attention of the class on the student who is responding to the question. Maintain eye contact with the student. Use nonverbal gestures to indicate your understanding, confusion, or support. Do not interrupt even if you think the student is heading toward an incorrect answer. On the frequent occasions when students do reach an incorrect answer, the other students may learn as much from that response as from a correct one. Furthermore, interrupting students does not create an atmosphere that encourages participation.

Call Students by Their Names

This avoids confusion as to who was called upon and also helps create a positive climate where students feel you know them as individuals.

Use Active Listening

Wait for a second or two following a student response, paraphrase when the answer is long, and check with the student to be sure your perception of his or her response is accurate.

Encourage Nonparticipants by Calling on a Specific Student to Answer a Question

Ask the question, then call on the student. If you call the student's name first, the rest of the class may not listen to the question. Another way to get all students to think of a response is to pose the question and tell students to raise their hands when they have an idea or response. Wait until all hands are raised before letting a student respond.

Randomly Select Students to Respond

Try not to follow any set pattern when calling on students.

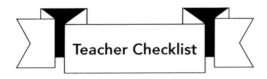

Teacher Checklist

Yes	No	
☐	☐	You planned your questions through discussion with peers, considering many questions and selecting those that would best stimulate student thinking.
☐	☐	You first asked a question of the class and then called on a student to respond.
☐	☐	You referred to students by name when calling on them and complimented them on a response.
☐	☐	You limited the use of closed-ended (information gathering) questions to instances when you clearly wanted students only to recall specific information or when you were starting students off in a discussion.
☐	☐	You used open-ended questions frequently to stimulate student thinking.
☐	☐	You used wait time (3-5 seconds) following a question to enable students to think about the question and responses.
☐	☐	You used positive nonverbal cues to show the importance of student responses and the interest you had in them.
☐	☐	You routinely probed student responses with additional questions to ensure they understood and to encourage them to think deeper.
☐	☐	You used techniques to engage all students in responding to questions.
☐	☐	You maintain a list of effective teacher questions to use in future lessons.

APPLICATION

Work-based Learning

Examples of Work-based Learning Strategies

There are a variety of work-based learning strategies. You should look at your school and community resources, the needs of your students, and the connections between your school-based learning and curriculum possibilities to find the appropriate strategy for your school. Some strategies, you will find, are appropriate for any class.

Field Trips

Trips to various workplaces give students opportunities to see firsthand a wide range of work environments. Prepare students before the trips with background information about the site, its business operations, etc. Students gain more from these experiences when they prepare questions beforehand. Questions can center on the workers' background, preparation, responsibilities, as well as the products/services provided by the business. Both younger and older students can benefit from the career exploration provided by field trips.

Job Shadowing

This involves a visit to a workplace during which the student follows an employee around. The student has an opportunity to see what the worker really does in his/her job. By observation and questioning, the student can almost feel as though he/she is in the position. Prior classroom preparation for the shadowing helps students connect the experience with academics, career pathways, related job skill requirements, and future education and employment opportunities. The length of time for shadowing can vary from one hour to a full day. Some common characteristics of job shadowing are:

- providing realistic views of specific jobs
- observing employees on the job
- questioning the employee shadowed
- completing related class activities

Mentoring

A mentor provides support and encouragement to a student at the worksite. This is a formally established relationship. Students learn rules, norms, and expectations of the workplace from mentors. They also gain valuable career insight and guidance based on the personal career experiences of their mentors. Mentors typically serve as resources to students; the mentor becomes a student's "other teacher," resolving personal and work-related problems, issues, and questions. Some common characteristics of mentoring are:

- including a learning activity beyond work responsibilities
- providing an experienced employee to serve as coach and advisor
- including career insights and showing how core academic skills relate to work success

Special Projects

On occasion, community agencies or employers have work projects that students can do. These might include creating a newsletter or brochure, conducting research, completing or assisting with a community survey, and planning committees. Students can work on these activities either at school, at the workplace or community agency, or on site of the project.

Structured Work Experiences

These work experiences take place at the workplace and are linked to a program of study by a specific curriculum that integrates school-based instruction with work-based learning. A written training agreement is drawn up between the school and the worksite, and student learning plans are designed to correlate coursework with work-based learning. Student progress in these programs is supervised and evaluated collaboratively by school and workplace personnel. These structured work experiences may be paid or unpaid and may take place in public, private, or nonprofit organizations. The employer is under no obligation to offer regular employment to the student following the work experiences.

There are four main types of structured work experiences strategies:

1. **Cooperative Education (Co-op):** This work-based learning experience includes structured work experiences that are directly related to the student's educational program. The school and the participating business organization develop training and evaluation plans as the student's course of study and the means to measure his/her progress and success. Co-op offers students an opportunity to extend the classroom into a workplace setting. These structured work experiences may be paid or unpaid and they usually carry academic credit for students. Co-op placements can be for a semester or over several semesters. It is important to ensure that the student's work experiences continue to lead toward new competencies and new workplace learning. This program requires a collaborate effort among the school, the employer, and the student. Characteristics of cooperative education include:

- Demonstrating relevant academic and technical skills
- Including an opportunity to achieve on-the-job knowledge and skills
- Providing students with on-the-job training by a competent employee
- Ensuring students are participating in a related academic or technical course

2. **Internships:** Under an internship, the student applies academic and technical skills in a work or simulated work environment. This program usually occurs near the end of a student's preparatory academic studies. The internship may be paid or non-paid. The term "practicum" is sometimes used in place of an internship. Characteristics of this program include:

- Arranging for students to observe work and the workplace
- Developing needed work competencies
- Targeting experiences to students' chosen career fields
- Providing an opportunity for students to learn work terminology, climate, and protocol

3. **Clinical Work Experience:** This type of work experience requires on-site supervision by a certified teacher. Typically, these experiences take place in the health field, where students practice and demonstrate skills learned in school-based programs in a real-world work-based setting.

4. **Supported Employment**: These work experiences require on-site supervision by a trained job coach or other personnel. Supported employment can take place in any environment. Students in these programs have disabilities or other needs for additional support on the job. Supported employment is a place/train/support model rather than a train/place/support model.

Service Learning

In this type of work-based learning strategy, students learn and develop skills through participation in organized community or human services. These service-related work experiences are:

- conducted in and serve the needs of a community
- coordinated between the community and the school
- integrated into the student's academic curriculum
- structured to provide time for students to reflect on their experiences
- opportunities to use acquired skills in real-life community based situations
- experiences that extend learning beyond the classroom and strengthen what is taught in the classroom
- a means to foster a sense of caring for others

Apprenticeships

These are formal systems of training in occupations that require a diverse range of skills and knowledge. Apprenticeships involve planned day-by-day experience training on the job. The program must be carried out under proper supervision. Students combine work on the job with school-based technical and academic courses related to the occupation having the apprenticeship. State and industry standards are norms for most apprenticeship programs.

School-Based Enterprises

Under this work-based learning strategy, students produce goods and/or services as part of their educational program. Typically, students manage a business of their own that sells goods. Enterprises may be located on or off the school site but are always a part of the school's program.

Organizational Structures for Implementing Work-based Learning Programs

Work-based learning may be organized in many formats. Some key structural dimensions that need to be determined are:

Location

On-campus or off-campus. Work is any activity that provides goods or services for other people. Numerous on-campus student activities could qualify as work. Examples include participation in school publications, musical performances, or dramatic productions; office work, cafeteria work, and running the school store. There are some practical advantages to offering the program on-campus. Fewer travel and insurance expenses are involved. Teachers have more control over the work activities and learning; they also can monitor more easily. If work placements in the community are difficult to find, a school-based enterprise may be an answer for providing work-based learning opportunities.

A significant advantage of an on-campus program is the ease of linking the work-based learning to the academic curriculum. However, off-campus may be the only environment in which students can acquire some knowledge or skill related to a particular occupation or industry. Also, learning to communicate and get along with co-workers of all ages, supervisors, and customers can more realistically take place at an off-campus worksite.

Supervision

By teachers or employers. To the degree that the work-based learning program is designed to meet academic competencies, participation by teachers is essential. Teachers cannot only supervise the student on the job but also assist in planning the student's work activities. If the purpose of the work-based learning program is more than improving student's academic achievement, then other adults should share in the supervisory responsibility.

Sharing responsibility for supervision is a defining feature of cooperative education. Job supervisors are important when the purposes of the program are to build students' generic work skills, personal and social competence, and understanding of an occupation or industry. The ideal is to have joint supervision. Just as some teachers lack knowledge about work and work skills, some worksite supervisors lack knowledge about education and school.

The key is correlating school and work-based learning. Collaboration between schools and outside employers can enhance the workplace knowledge of teachers and inform worksite supervisors about school curriculum requirements and components.

Time

During or after school hours. When students participate in the work-based learning experience may depend on the flexibility and attitudes of your school community. Time away from the school day competes with other academic learning. Thus, if the work-based learning program is to take place during the school day, good justification should be provided that the program accomplishes essential academic learning.

Programs such as career academics and clusters use work experiences or internships that may take from 19–20 hours a week for a year. These are typically scheduled outside school hours, which lessens time for other academic learning. Sometimes a co-op program is scheduled during school. This reflects confidence in the program's ability to enhance academic skills. If the program is slated during school hours, it could also reflect that school's commitment to career exploration, broad understandings of work and occupations, generic work skills, and preparing students for employment.

Compensation

Pay or school credit. A reward for work done is important. In work-based learning programs, there are many instances when students receive monetary compensation.

Employers are usually willing to pay students if the programs are directly tied to academic curricula that include acquiring knowledge and skill for a particular occupation or industry. An employer may also easily justify pay if the program develops students' personal and social competence and generic work skills. Usually, employers are not in favor of providing monetary compensation for career exploration experiences.

School-based enterprises sometimes provide scholarships for students upon graduation. Course credit is usually awarded and sometimes directly tied to a course that is linked to the work experience. For example, in co-op experiences, students receive a grade as a part of the course work for that course of study. In programs that combine academic and vocational curricula in career academies, clusters, pathways, and similar structures, academic credit is usually awarded. There are no definitive rules on whether a work-based learning program carries course credit or not and whether some programs guarantee monetary compensation. Ideally, if the design of the program is strong and if employer participation is possible, students should be paid and receive course credit. This would motivate students' performances and participation.

Participation

Individually or in groups. It is less cumbersome to design, plan, monitor, and evaluate group programs. Similar requirements for students engaged in a school enterprise, such as a school store, can be applied to groups of students. Career exploration activities can also be easily adapted to groups. When students engage in individual jobs through internships, co-op, etc., it is difficult to design/find work-related assignments that are appropriate for numbers of students. In these instances, assignments need to be customized for each student.

Considerations When Developing Work-based Learning Programs

To ensure the educational value of work-based learning opportunities, the following considerations should be noted when initiating a program.

Make Sure Students Are Ready to Work

Successful work experiences require the right attitude about work in general. Good work habits, social skills, and energy and enthusiasm for the work experience are predictors of student success.

Match Students to Social Context of Work

Students need to be carefully matched with worksites. Becoming familiar with the employer and his or her style is just as important as knowing the student. The experience should be one in which both the employer and the student's satisfaction are maximized.

Consider Size of Program

Some studies have indicated that small size and specific focus of work-based programs contribute to positive results. Being a part of a small group with adult attention and assistance seems to enhance student's success.

Connect School-Based and Work-based Learning

Efforts to ensure a connection between school-based learning (curriculum) and work-based learning are important; however, some research indicates that even when the connections are weak, students learn many valuable competencies and develop skills in the work-based learning activity. It is suggested that the effort to connect school and work is not as significant as the effort to ensure that authentic work experiences give students opportunities to apply knowledge in useful context. Thus, students gain a deeper understanding of their abilities and the opportunities they can create through education and experience. By this criterion, all programs have value, whether they explicitly connect to the school curriculum or not.

Assessing the Quality of Teaching and Learning at Work

The National Center for Research in Vocational Education recently completed a study of the quality of teaching and learning in work-based learning programs. This study outlined three aspects of the workplace environment that are significant factors in assessing the quality teaching and learning at work. These are:

1. the types of tasks students perform and the social context in which these tasks are established, accomplished, and processed

2. the influence of the community of practice—how it goes about teaching students what they need to know and how it defines the student's role

3. the training philosophy and practices for promoting learning at work

To assess the quality of teaching and learning, you must constantly look at the work place as a learning community. What is important is to have some way of knowing whether the program is accomplishing its desired purposes.

Teacher Checklist

Yes   No

☐   ☐   The work-based learning system benefits students, employers, the school, and the community.

☐   ☐   The knowledge and skills required in a course of study or curriculum are applied in a workplace as a part of the work-based learning program.

☐   ☐   Students receive either credit or monetary compensation for their participation in the work-based learning program.

☐   ☐   The work-based learning program provides career exploration and planning opportunities.

☐   ☐   Students increase personal and social competencies related to work as well as gain a broad understanding of an occupation or industry.

☐   ☐   Students engaged in worksite learning and programs are supervised by both an employer and an educator.

☐   ☐   There is regular communication between the employer and school staff to judge student progress.

☐   ☐   Students' attitudes and dispositions indicate work readiness.

☐   ☐   Students are matched appropriately to worksites.

☐   ☐   The work-based learning strategy(ies) implemented is appropriate for the school, students, and educators involved in the program.

☐   ☐   A strong partnership exists between cooperating employers and the school.